HERE WE **GROW**

HERE
WE
GROW

The Marketing Formula to 10x Your
Business and Transform Your Future

MARCIA BARNES

Published by Advantage, Charleston, South Carolina.
Member of Advantage Media Group.

ADVANTAGE is a registered trademark, and the Advantage colophon is a trademark of Advantage Media Group, Inc.

Printed in the United States of America.

10 9 8 7 6 5 4 3 2 1

ISBN: 978-1-64225-254-5 (Paperback)
ISBN: 978-1-64225-434-1 (eBook)

LCCN: 2022914950

Cover design by Joshua Cook.
Layout design by Matthew Morse.

This publication is designed to provide accurate and authoritative information in regard to the subject matter covered. It is sold with the understanding that the publisher is not engaged in rendering legal, accounting, or other professional services. If legal advice or other expert assistance is required, the services of a competent professional person should be sought.

Advantage Media Group is a publisher of business, self-improvement, and professional development books and online learning. We help entrepreneurs, business leaders, and professionals share their Stories, Passion, and Knowledge to help others Learn & Grow. Do you have a manuscript or book idea that you would like us to consider for publishing? Please visit **advantagefamily.com.**

Dedicated to my Father who showed us how to love and serve others. By doing so, he has become the greatest leader I've ever known. Love. Serve. Lead.

CONTENTS

INTRODUCTION

*No man ever steps in the same river twice, for it's not
the same river and he's not the same man.*

—HERACLITUS

L ife is nothing if not an ongoing series of transformations. We experience physical and emotional growth as we move from childhood to adulthood, then gradual changes as we age. The same is true for our life experiences, relationships, and careers. Circumstances, resources, interests, geography, climate, finances, connections—they all constantly change and bring us new opportunities to make decisions about how we will change next.

This is just as true in business as it is in life in general. Many people see the loss of a job or revenue as a problem that needs immediate remediation and miss the fact that they have just been given a push toward making new choices and embracing new opportunities. Although they might be difficult to see in the moment, they are there for you to seize and take advantage of the possibilities they offer. Everything you need is there in front of you. You just have to figure out how to put the pieces together. It may take more work, more learning, more trial and error—more changes. Then comes the hard part: gathering the confidence to move forward without fear. Every person has something valuable trying to get out of their heart and into the world or marketplace. And you are a lot more capable than you think.

I run a performance marketing agency that specializes in helping businesses be disruptive and attain sustainable, transformational growth. Some of the clients I've worked with didn't think they could grow their businesses or multiply their valuation by ten. Over the years, I've worked with marketers who thought their role wasn't important or worthy enough to be on an executive team. Some felt they didn't have the chops to build a glorious career multiplying several businesses. All of these things were well within their grasp.

Every person has something valuable trying to get out of their heart and into the world or marketplace.

The only thing standing in the way of their achievement of those goals was their belief that they couldn't do it. I knew it was more than possible because that's exactly what I have done for myself again and again throughout my life.

I am a farmer's daughter from rural Indiana and spent twenty-five years as a farmer's wife. My dad worked full-time as an engineer at Seagram's and tended our farm before and after his hours there as well as on weekends. Despite all the time my dad put in working, my family was poor. Like many children who grow up in poverty, my sisters and I also experienced abuse and the impact of addiction in the family. All the studies regarding poverty, abuse, and addiction say that if a child is raised in an environment with one or more of these things, the odds of getting out of that cycle of poverty are very low. Just by the merit of where we were born and who was in our lives, my sisters and I were set on a path from birth that should have led us to the same kind of lives and struggles our parents faced.

That's not the path we chose, however. Despite the traumas and lack of resources at home, we were blessed to have supportive influences in our lives. My grandparents were very involved with my sisters and me. We had 4-H leaders, sports coaches, and teachers who were invested in uplifting our hearts and minds. Those years were hard to get through. But they also enabled me to develop a resilient spirit that helped me navigate the ongoing impact of childhood abuse and trauma. Our father passed along his positive attitude, work ethic, and faith. Our mother taught us about independence and justice and instilled in us a love of learning. This enabled me to choose a path away from a broken life I was statistically more likely to build.

Although I studied journalism at Indiana University, I became a librarian. That hadn't been in my career plan, but I had learned how to run a library as an undergrad and continued with it as I got engaged and eventually married a man from my hometown. I was offered a job as a librarian at Xavier University to replace a woman who was going on maternity leave. My actual start date wasn't for five more months, so I had to find a way to make money in the meantime. I took a part-time job selling advertising over the telephone. In my first week, I broke the company sales record and made $1,500, which would be the equivalent of about $4,000 today. I was making more money than my father did as a full-time engineer and five times more than I was as a librarian.

This discovery changed my options for moving forward once again. I could make amounts of money I had never expected in sales and marketing, a profession that wasn't of particular interest in college. I liked the work, though, and I was really good at it, so I stayed with that company for a few years. When I was considering starting a family, I knew the commute would be too long to manage with children to take care of. But there were no local jobs that could provide the same kind of income. Again, I was faced with a choice: stay the course or explore new options. In this case, I chose to learn how to open my own marketing business close to home.

I was twenty-six years old when I started my first business. It was a telemarketing call center that employed mostly women on a part-time basis. This was in the 1980s when divorce rates were high, child support was low, and a lot of women were suddenly having to face raising and paying for children on their own for the first time. Choices were limited due to the types of jobs available and the hours they could spare to work, which were usually when school was in session. I had seen the impact this kind of situation could have when my sister became a single mom. She lost her home and her children and had to move in with my parents. I started to think that I could help these women by providing them with sales jobs where they could earn full-time pay with part-time hours. Working with a sales commission model, they would be able to pick up their kids from the bus stop and still make $40,000 to $80,000 a year.

This business gave me the first glimpse of the impact that transformational change can have on people. My team was made up of women who had been drowning in divorce debt and were trying to take care of their kids while working low-wage jobs with often inconsistent schedules. They were sacrificing raising their children the way they thought was best just to keep food on the table. With the money they earned from my call center, they were able to get out of debt, be home for their kids, buy cars and houses, and build strong families as single mothers. I found a deeply personal joy in being part of helping people transform their lives, and that has never left me.

After five years, I closed that business. I had other sales and marketing jobs in the years that followed. I experienced setback after setback. One company had a really big issue with sexual harassment (the norm in the 1980s). I was the first woman in my family to have a career outside of farming. I complained to my parents about two bosses I had trouble with. My mom asked me if I was flirting or wearing something attracting attention. Women were passed over for management jobs. The company wanted to hire a new person to fill a position that wasn't available yet, so they demoted me to frontline sales and gave my managerial job to the new guy. But I was the one he came to every day asking for help because he didn't know how to lead a sales team. Incompetent.

When I was pregnant with my youngest son, I left that company to work for a competitor. Ryan was born sixteen weeks early and weighed only one pound nine ounces. He spent ninety days in the neonatal intensive care unit, during which time I bounced back and forth between home, work, and the hospital. The more he developed, the more I understood that he was going to have some significant health challenges. The limited strength of his immune system and lungs wouldn't allow for him to stay in day care while I worked. With all of these new changes in my life and some dissatisfaction with the job I had, I decided to build a new path forward. I could start a home-based business that would allow me to hire a caregiver to help while I was working.

Instead of going alone into a new business, I took on a partner, Greg. That's when I learned that you should do some serious vetting of those you intend to work with before committing to anything. We built a small business selling advertising and were growing steadily. Then everything changed on one really bad day. Greg borrowed my car the night before the really bad day. Greg disappeared, along with the car I had lent him, all the money in the business account, and

5

the $3,000 deposit for the business phones. My car wound up in an impound yard after the police found it totaled on the side of the road. Greg's mother had been my babysitter, and she had disappeared as well. Greg had a drug addiction. Within the space of a few hours, I had lost everything, even the means to call my mom for a ride to the pediatrician for Ryan's two-year-old well-baby checkup. I had to ask a neighbor if she would let me use her phone.

The already disastrous day wasn't done with me yet. The doctor told me that afternoon that Ryan had cerebral palsy and would never walk. My mom dropped me off at home and left me there alone, holding my two babies. My mind was racing, repeating a constant refrain of failure: "Whenever I start to build something great, something else comes along and knocks everything down to the dirt." My life had been one endless series of being beaten down by circumstances and other people, only to pick myself up and move forward. Where had that gotten me? Kneeling on my living room floor, holding my babies, crying my eyes out, and praying for clarity and guidance.

In that moment, I needed God's help to see the possibilities in the utter ruin of my life. I thought and prayed on that floor until I realized that the central theme in all these problems was me. I was making bad decisions about who I was partnering with, working for, and trusting. I wasn't trusting my own capabilities and judgment. I wasn't trusting in the Lord to guide me toward the pathways that would transform my life from one of constant struggle to one full of success. Before I got up off that floor, I knew I was built for more than what I had allowed into my life to that point. I made a commitment to myself that I would spend every day developing my mind, talents, and experiences in ways that would empower me to move forward.

I was totally broke. I survived on government assistance food stamps for a short period of time and with the help of family and friends. But every day I did something to develop myself. I read and listened to books, connected with people who had gone down a path I wanted to model, and met others I could learn from. I put these new ideas and methods into practice, evaluated the impact they had, and decided whether or not to keep them in my toolbox of resources. The changes weren't noticeable right away. Over time, though, I realized that everything I had been doing was transforming how I worked, how I interacted with the world, how I raised my boys, and how I approached my life. Instead of bringing me to another place of ruin, this new pathway enabled me to be a strong role model for my kids and give them the lifestyle and education I wanted for them. More than that, though, I have been able to help bring transformational change to others.

My experiences in life have taught me that while change is inevitable, we all have the power to choose where we go from that turning point. My experiences in business have shown me that there are pathways to transformative growth that may not be easy to see when you work alone. But when you work with people who follow the data, have a supportive team mindset, and possess a genuine desire to help, the business results follow.

In this book, you'll see how my own transformational growth has led to an approach to performance marketing that relies on accountability and practices that show measurable results. What you're about to read may go against what you've always thought about sales and marketing. I challenge you to keep your mind open to the potential your own business has for achieving transformational growth as a result of the information presented in this book.

These are the practices we apply every day at Valve+Meter, both internally and with our clients. Our mission is to help businesses reach their full potential through profitable marketing programs that are scalable and repeatable. We show clients how to achieve transformational growth in their business outcomes, whether that applies to profitability, culture, team building, or any combination of things that impact a business's success in their field.

I've grown a company from $2 million in revenue to over $400 million. I've also grown a business unit from $0 to $50 million and another from $0 to $34 million. Clients at Valve+Meter have increased their value by ten times, tripled profitability, or scaled business. I've bought over half a billion dollars' worth of marketing over the years. I've helped grow thousands of jobs and promoted hundreds of leaders. If these are the results you're looking for, turn the page now.

PART 1

LOVE,
SERVE,
LEAD

CHAPTER 1

LEARN THIS FIRST

T here is something wrong with the way most people and businesses think about marketing. One of the most common ways that businesses determine how much to spend on marketing is to apportion a small percentage of gross revenues. The US Small Business Administration recommends that 7 to 8 percent of gross or prospective revenues be allocated for marketing costs if you have a business that takes in less than $5 million.[1]

The problem with taking a simple blanket percentage approach to creating marketing budgets is that there is a high likelihood of seeing less than optimal performance and overspending. Marketing then gets the blame for performance failings and is viewed as less important to the health of the business because it is a unit that spends money instead of making it. This is a mainstay of traditional business thinking that results in lost earning potential and wasted resources.

An Unlimited Budget for Marketing That Works

My philosophy is that there is an unlimited budget for marketing that works. You don't just watch the bucket of marketing spend and see

---

1   Caron Beesley, "How to Set a Marketing Budget That Fits Your Business Goals and Provides a High Return on Investment," Small Business Association, accessed January 7, 2021, https://www.sba.gov/taxonomy/term/15051?page=37.

how much money is being returned. You have to evaluate the things that you're doing in marketing and figure out which ones are driving revenue and which ones aren't. This comes only when you approach your marketing strategy in a way that focuses on specific, measurable results and finds the value that translates into the growth you want to see in your business.

I once spoke with a client who said that he had $1.7 million to spend on marketing for the coming year. His company has a goal of growing from $10 million in revenue to $15 million within a year, a sum that would be incredibly transformational. I said to him that we'd look at his business and goals before we figured out how much he needed to spend on marketing. I wanted to make sure that they were spending that money on marketing that drove the needed revenue to hit that specific goal. We would try some things, evaluate the impact, and then make adjustments. When we found the mechanisms and tactics that provided the best results, we would invest in expanding those things to ensure the growth they were looking for. The result was that he spent $800,000 and hit his goal.

I learned how powerful this approach to marketing worked when I took Dave Lindsey on as a client in 1999. I met Dave through a colleague in Texas who sold automated dialing equipment for robocalls. Dave owned a $2 million business called Defenders that sold home security systems. At the time, I co-owned a call center an hour and a half outside of Indianapolis. We specialized in cultivating leads for businesses, which were handed to their sales teams for conversion and charged clients per hour for our services. It turned out that Dave was in Indiana, too, and wanted to hire my company.

Dave was a real test-and-invest kind of person. He was thinking of investing in my colleague's robocall equipment but wanted to test it out first in my call center before making a full commitment. When he asked if I thought it would work, I said that some people are likely to never listen to the messages the system sent and that he could probably get more results using live telemarketers too. We ran the equipment for a few weeks, and it produced the right number of sales that resulted in the right amount of return. The problem was that there wasn't much volume, like I suspected, and there were more people who were upset at having received robocalls than who actually purchased.

Dave then hired my company to do another test: Could we generate thirty appointments for his salespeople? We settled on an hourly rate, and my team quickly secured the number of sales calls he requested. He then wanted to contract for another thirty appointments and then fifty appointments. It went on from there. We got his sales team really good leads, and within the first ninety days of working with Defenders, my team had grown the business from a $2 million to an $8 million run rate. Our relationship grew as well, until we provided the entire sales pipeline for his business while still remaining a vendor. This was my first real experience with fractional services in business and how much sense it makes to outsource some of your operations to people who specialize only in the areas you need.

How Defenders Changed Me Forever

Working with Dave was as transformational for me and my business as it was for his. He was strong in finance and process, whereas I was strong in leadership and developing people. We were both committed to learning and growing our skills. He dreamed the big dreams, and I got things done. These different perspectives allowed us to learn from each other. After doing some analysis, Dave approached me with a proposal to change how he paid for my company's services. He suggested that instead of paying per hour for making appointments, he would pay per appointment set, which would actually increase the amount of money he was paying for my marketing services.

Having a client suggest that they pay you more for your services may seem unlikely or an unwise business practice. But Dave thought that changing our payment model would also enable us to think in different ways, which would benefit both of our businesses. On my end, it would drive thought leadership and provide incentive to innovate ways for setting more appointments. At the time, I thought I was already providing as many high-quality leads as I could. I started thinking differently with this new variable pay model. The goalposts were being changed, so our approach would also have to change to keep as much money coming in as possible.

Being on a variable pay model worked for Dave's visionary way of thinking about the financial model to drive growth, even though he was paying more for marketing than he was before. When you pay an hourly rate for marketing, you are not guaranteed that the money you're spending is resulting in the maximum number of quality sales appointments. A marketer may talk to fifteen prospects in an hour but set only one or two appointments. Your cost for getting those appointments is the hourly rate divided by the number of actual meetings scheduled. The fewer appointments set, the more expensive your marketing spend. If you're only paying when an appointment is set, your marketing costs are directly linked to a sales call that has a high likelihood of converting into revenue. With this approach, you maximize the channel and can close sales more efficiently.

We tried this for six weeks, and my company went from earning $30 an hour to $85 an hour, which was two and a half times more than we'd been previously making from Defenders. Dave was happy to pay this much more because he was also seeing the same increase in appointments that led to sales. Moving from cost per hour to cost per acquisition boosted revenues all around and our businesses grew. The arrangement worked so well that we took it a step further. Instead of paying me per appointment set, Dave would pay per installation.

Now my team would get the leads and set the appointments. Dave's reps would sell the products to end users, and when his technicians completed the installation, I would get paid $250. This made Defenders' marketing spend even more efficient. When they were paying per appointment, a sale wasn't guaranteed. A sales rep may not close a deal, and the company would have paid for a service that didn't result in new revenue. I was a bit skeptical about this new approach because I would have to rely on Defenders' sales and installation staff to get paid. Since moving to a cost per acquisition model was working well, I agreed to give this new idea a try.

I'm very transparent with my teams, and I let them know that we were changing up the payment model for Defenders. Just as when we moved to getting paid per appointment, we all started thinking and seeing things differently. One thing that stood out to several people on my team was that sales reps were canceling or not going to appointments. We would get calls from customers or conduct confirmation and follow-up calls after an installation was scheduled. They would tell us that whoever was supposed to meet with them from Defenders either out-and-out canceled the meeting or never showed up.

I went back and forth with Dave and his vice president of sales for weeks, and there was little action being taken to address the issue on their end. My team had determined that about 40 percent of meetings were being classified as no-shows. That translated into throwing away 40 percent of my pay, Dave's revenues, and his salespeople's commissions. This was a huge amount of money being lost. I couldn't understand why this wasn't more of an issue for Dave or his sales team, which worked on a straight commission model. Why would they skip meetings when the result would be missing out on 40 percent more income?

We also found the root of the problem. In looking at the data on which appointments were kept and which weren't, a pattern showed that meetings scheduled for after 5:00 p.m. or on the weekend were the ones being blown off. Sales reps would close a few sales during the day and that was enough for them. They would rather sacrifice commissions than have to work after hours.

You treat your staff, partners, and vendors with integrity and respect. You help empower them to grow and succeed, and in turn you do as well.

As the weeks went by, I grew more frustrated. It was obvious that Dave wasn't taking the situation seriously enough. My revenues were being impacted, but more than that, if you know that the person you're serving is missing out, you're especially required to get that point across, right? I have always taken a service approach to business. You treat your staff, partners, and vendors with integrity and respect. You help empower them to grow and succeed, and in turn you do as well. Up until this point, that was the kind of relationship I had with Dave. He was genuinely invested in the well-being of my team and business. On this issue, though, he wasn't listening.

When I walked into his office for the fourth time to address the situation, he was behind his desk wearing a brand-new Plantronics headset. This was the latest in high tech gear for call centers, and Plantronics was top of the line. I asked him what he had, and he started gushing about its bells and whistles. I asked him how much it cost. He said $250, which was a lot of money then and exactly what he paid me for every installation. I asked if I could see it for a minute, then turned to leave the office with it in my hands.

"Where are you going with that?" he asked.

"I'm going out to the parking lot," I replied coolly and calmly. "I'm going to put it under my car and drive back and forth over it until it's broken into a thousand pieces, because that's exactly what your sales reps are doing to my leads."

This finally got his attention. Sometimes you need to be bold enough to make your point in a way that can be heard and demonstrated. He may have been okay with losing out on 40 percent of potential sales, but since my business was dependent on his sales, I was not. It wasn't just the loss of money for myself and my team; it was also bad business from a marketing, vendor relationship, customer relationship, and reputation perspective. It was simply the right thing to fight for.

Dave asked me what I wanted him to do. I proposed a new system of checks and balances that his sales reps would have to comply with. When we got calls from customers saying that a sales rep never showed up, I would take that back to Defenders. The salesperson would counter by saying that they went but that the customer wasn't there. This new system would make it easier to verify whether the sales rep actually went to their appointments. As you can imagine, many of the sales staff weren't happy with this change in procedures, but they complied anyway. Soon we recovered about 75 percent of leads that had been a problem before and found that the remaining were legitimate cases of no-show customers or cancellations. Dave was pleased to win back the lost revenue.

The Flywheel Effect

I learned a lot during these years with Defenders. The most important is that if you want to use marketing for business growth, you should be looking at cost per acquisition instead of budgets based on percentage of revenues. When the money you spend on a marketing activity or resource leads directly to producing revenue, you can measure the effectiveness of your tactics and strategies. Marketing also moves away from being a cost center for the business to become a revenue generator.

The second lesson I learned was that it takes not just one person or business unit to get the performance measure you're looking for. You are really working with a flywheel effect. In his book *Good to Great*, Jim Collins describes how businesses develop, grow, and succeed because of more than a single element. Businesses work like a flywheel system. There is stored energy in a flywheel. You need to expend a great deal of energy to make a heavy flywheel begin to turn. But the more you get it to turn, the more the momentum of the motion keeps it turning. You eventually reach a point when it spins faster and faster, with the same strength or energy spent as you did for the first turn.[2]

It takes everybody doing their part and holding each other accountable for their role in the business to achieve any kind of transformational growth.

Now apply that concept to a business. You invest in marketing to create leads for the sales team. Sales creates orders for operations, which executes the orders and then gets paid. Finance spins off profit, pays the bills, and reinvests in marketing. The more programs you can find that hit the right return on marketing spend (ROMS), the faster the flywheel can go without expending additional resources. Each unit plays a crucial role in keeping the business momentum moving toward transformational growth.

---

2   Jim Collins, "The Flywheel Effect," accessed January 7, 2021, https://www.jimcollins.com/concepts/the-flywheel.html.

What happens a lot of the time is that marketing is doing things that have a great deal of potential to work, but the sales team is not closing at the right rate or selling at a high enough revenue per deal. Cost per acquisition goes up, which impacts the Return on Marketing Spend (ROMS). Sometimes operations falls apart on answering calls, keeping customers satisfied, or completing work. Maybe the company is getting bad reviews online and operations isn't handling them appropriately. These can cause wrinkles in the cycle as well.

It takes everybody doing their part and holding each other accountable for their role in the business to achieve any kind of transformational growth. Marketing departments often take the blame when sales are slow or not meeting goals. There aren't enough leads. The leads aren't good. The leads are too big or too small. Based on these perceptions, which may or may not be accurate, revenues go down and so do the marketing budgets. When you hold every person and business unit accountable for their actions and roles in generating revenues, you don't tend to point performance issues back to the marketing department all the time. Instead, you get greater efficiency and incoming revenues for your marketing spend.

I know firsthand that this strategy works. It's the cornerstone of our approach to servicing clients at Valve+Meter. It was also the process that we set up and executed at Defenders and that grew the company from a $2 million business to one creating more than $400 million in revenue by the time I was ready to move on.

TOOLS FOR GROWTH

WORKSHEET: FLYWHEEL ASSESSMENT

Scan the QR code or visit mathbeforemarketing.com/flywheel

MY IDEAS FROM THIS CHAPTER

CHAPTER 2

PERMISSION TO LEAD

think I learned most of what I know about leadership by working in my family's garden when I was growing up. My mom saw working in the garden more as a punishment for me and my sisters when we had done something wrong rather than as a normal chore. She would watch our work from a lawn chair set along the edge of the garden and yell at us. "You're doing it wrong, you stupid, lazy kids!" And if you've never spent a day getting up and down on your knees digging in the dirt, let me tell you that it is hard work.

Working with my dad was a completely different experience. He would hoe right beside us, showing us how to use the blade correctly and make the work easier, stressing the importance of making sure we got rid of the potato bugs as we went along. Dad would cast a vision for us about what the potato crop would look like with or without those bugs and weeds. He was cheerful in the work and encouraged us, making the time we spent in that garden something we could almost enjoy.

From these experiences, I learned that my mom loved being a boss and that my dad loved the work. Mom liked having dominion over other people. That came through not only in how she treated my sisters and me but also in the amount of work we put in as a result. We never wanted to work with our mother because it really was a punishment. We knew we were just going to get a hell of a mess, which, unfortunately, is the way many people approach leadership and business.

As a farmer, my dad loved the work. That came through loud and clear in his approach with us in the garden and how we responded. He had dominion over the work itself, and because he loved it, he invited us to experience it with him while he led the way. My heart was filled more by working with my dad. We would do anything for him. We'd shovel manure, herd the cattle, castrate pigs ... whatever. We liked doing the work with him. He showed me that leadership follows easily when you love the work, serve the best interests of both the business and the people you work with, and gain permission from people to lead.

This philosophy is ancient wisdom. Every major faith has basic tenets that point to loving, serving others, and being humble as a way of life. It's also central to building a strong and prosperous business. A focus on having dominion over others and trying to raise ourselves up over one another doesn't draw people in. It doesn't inspire them to give their best discretionary effort. However, when we love people well, we develop a desire to serve them. When people feel us serving them and loving them well, they give us permission to lead them. And when we have permission to lead, we get transformational results. This is the foundation of my approach to business: love, serve, and lead.

Lessons in Leadership from Defenders

I had worked with Defenders as a contracted vendor for several years before Dave and I merged our two companies together. My team had been delivering marketing results that had exponentially grown Defenders' business. My relationship with Dave and my belief in his compelling vision made me confident that the move would benefit everyone involved. I became the company's director of marketing.

My group had always been separate from Defenders' sales team and under my leadership, while the sales team had its own leadership that I would work with either through Dave or directly. This divide had caused issues in the past, such as learning that my team was losing out on 40 percent of potential income due to missed sales calls when I was still a vendor. I had fought to show Dave that the issue was real, what the cause was, and how it could be fixed. It eventually was, but it was difficult to do as an external vendor. Once I was a part of the organization, I was in a better position to see the cross functionality between sales and marketing firsthand. I was also able to see that there were many internal cultural and operational conflicts that were impacting growth.

In many businesses, there is a rift between marketing and sales groups. The purpose of marketing is to drive potential customers to the sales department. The sales team is responsible for converting those potential customers into paying ones. Marketing departments are often seen as a drain on company revenue because money is spent to generate those sales leads. Sales departments are seen as a profit center because they close the sales, which results in revenue flowing into the company.

Marketing's role in enabling sales teams to make their numbers is often questioned. I've heard it all: There aren't enough leads coming from marketing. There are too many leads for us to realistically handle. The leads we get aren't good and waste our time. The leads we get result in spending too long with prospects and I can't close enough sales in a day. If a sales team isn't making their numbers, marketing is blamed. If they exceed their numbers, marketing doesn't get any credit.

This more traditional thinking toward the sales and marketing relationship has never sat well with me, so I chose not to subscribe to it. It doesn't allow for a mentality of love, serve, and lead and can breed a toxic culture, which does not benefit anyone. I had always approached running my teams from the perspective of enabling everyone involved to prosper, both personally and professionally. And it's this approach that allowed me to see things differently within Defenders, then advocate for cultural and procedural changes in ways that empowered others and got results.

As I began to establish the marketing group, I made adjustments to enable us to work within the larger organization. One thing that started to emerge was the importance of the learning and development systems for teams. Defenders had split human resources into two focuses. The administrative aspect dealt with payroll, benefits, legal issues, etc. The "fun" aspect included culture, training, events management, etc. Those who worked on the administrative HR responsibilities reported to the chief financial officer, and I ran the leadership and development team. The thought there was that I had leadership and development skills and that a lot of what this team did was internal marketing of the business to its own people.

Once all of the training group was reporting to me, I began hearing about things they would notice within the different sales units. The first was that sales and call center teams often differed in how they operated. There was a lack of uniformity and application of policies, commonality in issues, and other aspects of doing business that allowed us to have conversations about how to get the numbers to work better.

I also started to look at the business in terms of operational efficiency. Dave recommended that I read *The Goal: A Process of Ongoing Improvement*, by Eliyahu M. Goldratt. It discusses ongoing process improvement and is directed at factories. However, I found its principles to be applicable to our sales processes because it talks about looking critically at your business to find areas that could be changed to either generate more revenue or cut waste.

One important idea is that in a bad factory, you have a lot of scrap. You're wasting dollars and opportunities to impact your bottom line. A prospect calling into your business is now, in factory terms, a work in progress. If the call goes unanswered, it is scrap. You paid for marketing and did not convert the call into revenue. A missed sale is scrap. A good factory has low amounts of work in progress and very little scrap. A bad factory has piles of work in progress and a lot of scrap.

A good factory has low amounts of work in progress and very little scrap. A bad factory has piles of work in progress and a lot of scrap.

For example, in a call center, not answering calls is scrap because you paid for the marketing already and wasted the call by not answering it. Let's say that you're dropping one thousand calls (this is more common than you think). If revenue per call is $100, you've lost $100,000 in revenue. This adds up fast because you're already paying the overhead and marketing cost, so recovering these calls is a contribution margin impact. If your gross margin is 40 percent, then you've lost $40,000 in profit. Many businesses will miss fixing this because they didn't want to add another person to answer the call, even though the cost of hiring one person might create ten times their wages in profit.

Understanding this concept of scrap and how to recover it was central to how I made my career at Defenders. I started to see opportunities everywhere in the business. For example, the sales team and call center reported that 10 percent of their calls were from prospects who spoke only Spanish. Since we didn't have any bilingual reps, we lost out on that potential revenue. I recruited a group of bilingual salespeople and assigned them to handle those calls. Our revenue increased by 10 percent, which went straight to the bottom line because we had already covered all of our costs and overhead. It was found money. And there were a dozen different things like that we could address in a similar way.

This example was one of many where I could see an overlap of efficiencies among departments. My job was to use marketing to keep the company growing. But I recognized that if there were changes made by both sales and marketing, I could hit my goals easily and everyone could benefit. Dave was a huge proponent of implementing change after a test period where the results could be assessed through data. Change is never easy to embrace, and with the Defenders team, I had learned that the best way to effect change was to show Dave how the solutions were making the company more money. I could see the business processes and results that had a lot of waste in them. This enabled me to go in and solve a problem and then recover lost opportunities for profitability.

My team was running a marketing program that was producing a massive number of inbound online leads. By traditional thinking, that should be a great success. The sales team didn't think so. The feedback sales had was that a lot of the leads were bad and didn't result in sales. The data backed this up in that it was showing that I wasn't reaching my ROMS numbers. One day I was in one of the call centers and noticed that a few reps had stacks of papers on their desks. When I asked them what the papers were, they said they were the internet leads from my inbound marketing campaign. I asked if they had followed up on the leads and was told that they could only get to them when their phones weren't ringing with prospects calling in for sales help. The sales rep would make one or two attempts and stop.

What was happening was the sales reps were stalling on trying to connect with the inbound leads when delivered in print form. Instead, they found it more efficient to wait on the phone to ring and have a live person to sell to. You could call it lazy, but it's their own type of efficiency management and was representative of the common habits within the sales departments. Expectations as to what was acceptable and methods for hitting numbers can work against a business getting its best performance. It was hard to get the sales leader to listen when I pointed out that they were losing 40 percent of potential sales by skipping sales calls. He was a smart person with a smart excuse— the leads were bad. Trying to convince him to convince his team to make more attempts was difficult, and when he did it, the result was nominal.

As a last-ditch effort, I asked one of my receptionists to do a test for me. We sent all the internet leads to her, and she called them. When she got the customer on the phone, she transferred it to sales, who would then handle closing the sale. Overnight, we started hitting that ROMS, and the campaign that had seemed to be losing money began working. I found the inefficiency. When salespeople were handed a lead, they would try to reach out once or twice. When unsuccessful, they would throw it in a pile and forget about it, which is part of the sales culture in lots of businesses. If it takes an average of eight attempts to reach a prospect who converts, the numbers don't make it worth a salesperson's time when they can wait for the phone to ring and get low-hanging, high-converting fruit.

Coming in and telling the sales team that they have to operate differently wasn't going to be received well, let alone implemented with any measure of success. Knowing this, I tried a different solution that engaged my team in marketing. Building an entire inbound marketing team of administrative assistants responsible for outbound calling to connect to those internet leads and pass them to the sales team was so much easier than enacting new policies that wouldn't be well received. The process also allowed my team to prequalify leads so that if the prospect wasn't qualified, we did not transfer the lead to the sales team. We set up the salespeople for higher conversion rates and greater success.

Bringing Sales and Marketing Together

The changes I was making within my own group, based on learnings from other departments and interactions with people in the call centers and on sales teams, were proving to be successful. All of our numbers were climbing, and profits kept increasing as marketing became more entrenched in the organization. After the new inbound marketing team had been speaking with prospects for a while, one of the admins who handled some of the calls told me that she'd noticed many people didn't want a salesperson to come to their home. At that time, a customer would schedule an appointment for a salesperson to visit their home, recommend products, and close sales with a signed service contract. That visit was then followed with an installation by a technician.

While this was the industry standard for many years and we followed it, we didn't realize that it could be off-putting for a decent percentage of potential customers. "Marcia, these people really don't want a salesperson to come out," Carol on the admin team told me. "They've had an incident. There's something going on in their neighborhood. They're scared, and most of them don't want to see a salesperson. They want a technician out there to install the equipment. Don't you think we should just schedule the tech to go?"

It was a fair point, so I discussed the idea with Dave. He was of the mind that the company was doing really well with the approach they had always taken and that it was how everybody else did it, so there was no good reason to make a drastic change. He didn't like the idea of our call center reps closing a deal and the technicians getting the contract signed when they installed. Technicians, too, might not be happy about having to sell during their home calls, since that's not what they were hired to do. But I knew there was something to this idea, and we had a handful of technicians whom I knew were capable enough to close sales. I convinced Dave to let me take the next ten leads that came in, close the sale on the phone, and schedule installation for techs visiting the homes.

When Defenders got ten inbound calls, the sales team would close an average of three. Out of the ten calls to which my team of three technicians was assigned, we got seven sales. When we increased the number of calls to thirty, we encountered some hiccups but still had a huge uptick in closed sales. Dave was happy with the increase in sales and the success of the strategy, but he wasn't ready to implement a sweeping change throughout the company. Instead, we assigned two of the call center reps to make the sale and three technicians to install their sales and help create the best practices.

The team was so successful that we ended up expanding it into a whole branch in Chicago, where we got some pushback from the technicians. They liked it when the sales team provided them with signed contracts and all they had to do was the installation. That's what they were hired to do, after all. What do you do in this case? Push forward and force new policy on people who don't want to hear it? That wasn't the right path in my opinion, especially because I knew that it would not generate results and had a high likelihood of having a negative collateral effect on morale, job performance, and efficiency. Here is where we needed permission to lead.

Instead, we brought the Chicago techs and their management to meet with my sales team for a focus group / think tank session.

My goal was to figure out how to make this work to the benefit of everyone involved. Initially, we were barraged by the technicians for an hour straight. They said that we were lying about the sales, that we were cheating them, and that it was terrible to have to sell product in addition to performing the installations. Then one tech, Chris, stepped up and commanded the attention of the room.

"I don't know what you guys are complaining about," he said. "If I know that both homeowners will be there, I have the right address and the right phone number, and the credit card is processed, I never have any trouble installing the system. All I need is those four pieces of information to seal the deal."

After Chris finished speaking, I called a break and talked to the sales team. Could they get the four conditions Chris mentioned every time they spoke to a prospect? They told me that was exactly the information they were already getting. When we reconvened the meeting, I said that my team would ensure that every technician got those four details every time.

"Once the deal is sold, we're going to pass it to a manager to verify that the customer understands these four things and that we have the information correct before we send it to you," I told them. "If you get to the home and you don't think these things have been done, we can access the recording to double-check." This would hold everyone accountable for their part of the program, and once it was implemented, this new way of doing things worked. It was so successful, in fact, that we expanded it throughout the entire company, and the program became a big differentiator for Defenders in the market. All of the other home security companies said that you had to have a salesperson in the home to close sales, and we proved that you didn't.

After showing Dave that I was getting consistent improvements by working with sales to suggest things that would boost their numbers and solving for things that fixed my marketing campaigns, he put me in charge of both departments. It was much easier to get wins when sales and marketing were together and when the person running them was holding both teams equally accountable. That's when we started to become extremely efficient and gain more growth. The change wasn't readily accepted, though, from those who were entrenched in the culture that had been established long before I came along, which made leading with love all the more difficult and essential.

Gaining Permission to Lead

Much of the progress that was made during this time was a matter of bringing the sales staff together to work the existing leads better, rather than simply looking to increase the volume coming in. The more value I could squeeze out of the marketing campaigns, the more marketing we could buy. This meant addressing the bottlenecks for the sales group. This had been producing consistent wins since my early days working with Defenders. Business results were better when both sales and marketing were reporting to me. I was a good partner to the sales team and could influence them in my role as the leader of the marketing group. When both teams reported to me, though, I could work out the nits in between and

The only way to effectively lead is to have buy-in from your team— freely given permission to lead them.

hold them each accountable, and the results spiked from that. It caused us to think of ways we could convert deals at a higher close rate while still adding new marketing campaigns consistently.

Although the results generated by my approach were increasing the paychecks of the existing sales team, some were not on board with the model. It meant that things would have to change, and the natural human response to change is to push back. The only way to effectively lead is to have buy-in from your team—freely given permission to lead them. The team knew that I was genuinely interested in their success as much as I was in our business outcomes. They also knew that I wouldn't ask them to do anything that I wouldn't do myself. Having this kind of leadership inspired them to come to work every day and not only bring their best but also go above and beyond.

Establishing this kind of culture within a team or organization is essential to gaining any kind of growth. If I love and serve our people well, they give me permission to lead them, and we get transformational results. If the manager on our team loves and serves their team well, they will get better results. Put yourself in the shoes of an account manager for a client. If you and your team love and service the account well, over time the customer gives you permission to lead them to greater success. This converts into more revenues because the more growth you are delivering through this approach, the more the customer will invest to sustain that growth.

I loved and served the interests of my team and Defenders as a whole. My efforts gained permission from Dave and the team I built in the newly formed sales and marketing department to lead them forward into sustainable and repeatable growth. The successes impacted everyone both personally and financially. But there is also a part of this philosophy where I give others permission to lead. This happens when someone loves and serves our common cause enough to step out of their day-to-day routine or adherence to the status quo and enact some kind of change or draw attention to something they think is important.

Sometimes it's a frontline person who says, "Hey, I'm paying attention to this thing over here, and this is what I'm seeing." When people do that, they show that they have enough love for me and our cause and are serving well enough to have a candid conversation that might not necessarily be popular. I value those people, most especially because I'm one of them. I always had that drive when I worked for Defenders. I saw things differently, and I knew that what I had to say was out of love and in service to the organization. I wanted Defenders and everyone who worked there to be as successful as they could be. So I spoke my mind and brought up the things that others were not always happy to hear. People who are unafraid to do this are some of the most valuable people in the organization, so I give them permission to lead me to a solution.

What results from this style of leadership and business growth is that you create a dynamic movement of love, service, and transformation throughout your whole organization. It impacts everyone you touch, including your community partners, vendors, clients, internal team members, and networks of influence. I often have a young professional join my team early in their career. Within a couple of weeks, they inevitably ask some form of the question, "When do I get to be somebody's boss?" It reminds me of my mother sitting on the side of the garden while my sisters and I dug up potatoes all those years ago. Then I channel my father: if you focus on mastery over the work, you'll have all the leadership opportunities you'll ever want because you will become the kind of person who gains permission from others to lead them forward. And I firmly believe Zig Ziglar's quote that "You can have everything in life you want, if you will just help other people get what they want."

This was certainly true of my experiences with Defenders. Sticking with my beliefs for achieving transformational growth delivered for the company year after year. I was also given increasing numbers of leadership opportunities and responsibilities. I moved from heading the sales and marketing teams to becoming the chief marketing officer and eventually the CEO. Throughout the course of my tenure, Defenders grew into a $400 million business, with thousands of employees across multiple states. But all good things must come to an end.

I had spent more than fourteen years with Dave and Defenders when I started thinking about moving on. I'm an entrepreneurial spirit, and I was feeling a calling to go back to my roots. I like growing businesses. I like growing a business that I've worked for. But I really love growing other people's businesses, growing jobs, and helping people attain things that they've not ever been able to attain in the past. I felt it was time to strike back out on my own and create a business to do just that.

TOOLS FOR GROWTH

PODCAST: GETTING PERMISSION TO LEAD YOUR EMPLOYEES

Scan the QR code or visit mathbeforemarketing.com/culture

TOOLS FOR GROWTH

HARVESTING IDEAS

MY IDEAS FROM THIS CHAPTER

CHAPTER 3

TRANSFORMATIONAL RESULTS

E verything I have gone through in my life has shown me that our journey on this earth is one of continual transformation. I had gone from living in poverty as a farmer's daughter in rural Indiana to making record-breaking sales for a local advertising company. I'd opened and closed my own business, where we had empowered single mothers and women to build stable lives for themselves on their own. I had lost everything one horrible day and found myself kneeling on my living room floor facing a choice between succumbing to circumstances or fighting to find my own power. And I helped build a new business that led me down a path of learning, winning, and creating financial outcomes beyond my expectations.

Each of these stages in my life transformed me in some way. My years working with clients and growing Defenders sharpened my business acumen to focus marketing—and business practices in general—on achieving transformational growth. The combination of a solid product produced in consistent processes by people who love and serve was powerful.

After fourteen years of using my knowledge, skills, and talents to grow a single home security company and those who worked for it, I felt it was time to help others. I had been thinking for a while of starting a marketing agency that would combine my love, serve, lead philosophy with a system of data-driven marketing that produces sustainable growth. It took some time to figure out an exit strategy from Defenders and chart a course down this new path. But once I made the decision, Valve+Meter was born.

My goal was to take what I love to do—grow businesses—and do it the only way I know how. We would work with empirical data, build scalable programs and strategies, conduct tests regularly to ensure that what we were doing was generating both the ROMS and the growth that was planned, and verify that our work was transforming our clients in some way. I would infuse my agency with the love, serve, lead mentality and teach that to my team so that they could pass it on to their own teams and then to our clients. Together, we would change the way businesses think about how they buy marketing.

Redefining Marketing for Transformational Growth

For a long time, I had noticed a problem with the way marketing is bought and sold. Small to midsize companies either have an in-house marketing department or outsource the whole or portions of their marketing to agencies. In-house teams tend to be staffed with a fraction of the number of people with the specific skills necessary to impact growth. You would need experts in prospecting, digital marketing, print marketing, social media, website development, search engine optimization (SEO) … and the list goes on.

No one person has mastery of every discipline required for effective marketing, yet in-house teams are usually funded to have as few people on staff as possible, and the onus of performing all these tasks falls on their shoulders. This makes a marketing department into a cost center, not a profit center. It also results in expending much more time and energy to achieve a fraction of the performance that a highly skilled external team can deliver.

Marketing agencies can provide businesses with people who have the exact skills and experience they need to make their marketing activities more efficient. However, many agencies tend to want to sell the product they produce or what's got the highest gross margin in it for them, regardless of whether their clients are getting any real business results in return. They want to talk about impressions and cost per lead or cost per click. All these things are either leading indicators or just vanity metrics that don't mean anything without really measuring the ROMS.

Companies buying into this mentality have been conditioned to think this way by traditional marketing and business education. Agencies reinforce this by the way they sell marketing. Businesses also see their competitors doing things in the marketplace and growing. Or maybe they hear about things like SEO, search engine marketing, and social media marketing. Without knowing how these tactics work or what the benefits might be to their business, they want to use them simply because they're new or their competitors are using them. It's a copycat mentality that is based on the premise that if it's working for others, it should work for me. The thing these companies miss is some kind of measurement that shows definitively whether these tactics are working and what the direct impact is on their bottom line.

Many of the clients I've worked with feel like they've got to do SEO as well as have paid media, a website, and social media accounts. They're looking for a package deal that includes all these things, almost like a menu when you grab fast food on your way home from work. That menu is not giving them the ability to measure what's working, invest in the things that are generating increases in revenue, and cut the parts that aren't. I think many people buy marketing from a menu because it's quick and easy, just like with fast food. You know you shouldn't do it. It's going to make you feel like crap when you're done. It's not in line with your diet and health goals. But you pick something off that menu just to get immediate gratification.

When I was creating a vision for my agency, I wanted to build a place that would help businesses understand the power that marketing has in driving revenue and that a data-driven methodology is the way to achieve growth. Sounds logical, right? The challenge I started seeing shortly before I left Defenders, and definitely afterward, was that businesspeople have trouble believing this works. People would ask me for advice on their marketing or how we were doing it at Defenders. I would explain the ROMS methodology to them, and they just would shake their heads and say, "That's not how it's done."

This was so odd to me. I was openly sharing what I do at the request of strangers and even competitors, but they wouldn't believe that was how I was getting the success I was for my company. Then I started to realize that the way people buy and agencies sell marketing is broken and that was averse to what my methodology was about. I felt like there was a need in the marketplace, not only for growing a business and making money but also to bring justice, transformation, love, and servanthood back into marketing.

I had this strong desire to help other businesses create abundance, and I used that as the basis for developing Valve+Meter. Our whole approach focuses on ROMS and transformational growth. What these two metrics are differs from client to client. Transformation is not about getting all the way to the end result. Transformation is what we become at each part in the journey. For example, a company I work with came to me with $2 million in revenue. They needed to get to $3 million to become profitable, which was not a big jump. I knew how to get them to $3 million easily within about eight months.

That $1 million in growth was the transformation the business needed then, and I helped them achieve that goal. However, they thought that getting to $5 million was beyond the realm of possibility at the time. They had been beaten down in this $2 million spot for so long that they couldn't see themselves getting there, let alone beyond that number. But I could see it and have been working with them to get to $5 million in revenue over two or three years, which will be another huge transformation for them.

I have another client that is a fourth-generation business trying to go to the fifth generation. Their revenues have been stuck at $5 million for the past six years, and they couldn't figure out how to break through that barrier. To be in a position to pass that company on to four children, they would have to hit revenues between $10 million and $12 million. I knew exactly what to do to get them there within three years, and each step of that is a transformation. We also work with a $3 billion water utility whose main objective is to improve their net promoter scores (NPS). While the key performance indicator (KPI) for this client is not ROMS, our process still guides the outcome, and we achieved a 200 percent increase in NPS for them in one year.

Because transformational growth means different things to different businesses, I wanted to make sure to build a process that would combine what we know works with a client's specific needs. We take the time to learn about our clients, including their internal and external business, competitive landscape, marketing costs, goals, and other data, so that we can create a clear picture of what transformation looks like for them. Then we build strategic plans that set benchmarks, performance estimates, a schedule for testing tactics and analyzing results, and a flywheel strategy that only runs programs proven to deliver the right results based on our tests. This approach is where the name for our agency comes from.

If you think of marketing spend as a flow of energy through your business, you can add valves anywhere in that system. Some valves turn up growth when you open them. You can slow growth by turning a valve back down. You also need a meter to measure the results that come from the marketing spend that your valves let out. The meter needs to be continually checked because what was working six months or six weeks ago might not still be working today. My team collaborates with businesses to help them focus their open valves on actions resulting in growth and turn off the valves creating waste. We show them the metered results regularly to assess what, if anything, needs to be adjusted, if goals are being met, whether growth is on track, and what next steps must be taken.

It took me a few years to mold my vision into a viable agency, but in the spring of 2017, Valve+Meter officially opened its doors. I knew some great marketers, and I assembled a team to start the business with the intention of going after clients for whom we could build measurable results. For our first clients, we were looking for businesses where our model could fit. Of course, I had a pretty big network in Indiana to start with, but we also began building networks of contacts and relationships across the country. One of the opportunities I thought I saw was in the home services industry, which we already knew a lot about from my and our team members' past experiences. We were also getting a number of people in business-to-business sectors asking us to help with marketing, so we started to focus on those two things.

The Pivotal Role of Culture

We've built Valve+Meter from the ground up, with a heavy focus on culture. Our vision, methodologies, and values are very different from those of other marketing agencies and businesses in general. I have an overall goal of growing a client's business to ten times its valuation. I also want all our team members to be able to chart a path to a C-level position in their career. I want them to flourish personally, professionally, and financially; feel free to add to the exchange of ideas; and have a sense that they accomplish something important with their work. It's this kind of environment that results in the best efforts of everyone involved and drives the transformational growth at the heart of our mission at Valve+Meter.

You want to have a great culture in your business. It helps make what you do sustainable and repeatable, but it's also the right thing to do.

I'm always overwhelmed by how many businesses I see defining their culture like this: "We have a Christmas party, do awards recognition once a year, have a family picnic day, and complete a service project together." Those are events that have happened within your culture. And while they're certainly part of your culture, they don't define it. A company's culture is every conversation, team member, customer, vendor, and influencer who's helping you outside of your business. It's in how you hire, fire, promote, recognize, and affirm. It's how you choose to grow yourself and your leaders. It's all of it together—that "people part" of your business—that defines its culture.

You want to have a great culture in your business. It helps make what you do sustainable and repeatable, but it's also the right thing to do. Creating a clearly focused and supportive culture better engages team members and helps businesses be more successful. Research conducted by Gallup in 2017 found that 51 percent of the US workforce isn't engaged with their jobs and that companies with high rates of employee engagement are 21 percent more profitable.[3] Why is this? People who like coming to work and get some kind of fulfillment from it are more productive. They come up with more ideas, are more careful and avoid accidents on jobsites, and reduce waste. It's crazy the difference those numbers make. When you apply all those levers to the whole of a business, it's really difficult to say that you don't need to pay attention to culture and that you can just grow blindly.

Love, serve, and lead are at the heart of Valve+Meter's culture, and we attract team members who not only are comfortable with our philosophy and approach to marketing but also who thrive in this kind of environment. Our teams get to go home at the end of the day and say to their friends and families that their work did the following:

- Saved 20 percent of the jobs in a business
- Contributed $190,000 of revenue to another business
- Solved a problem for a family who owns a business and grew its value times ten
- Increased the valuation of a company, expanding its access to capital and enabling it to participate in acquisitions that are creating more jobs for people

These are big, big things to accomplish for a company as an individual. Yet most businesses don't talk to their people about those things or give them feedback on what the results mean. So it's easy for team members to get caught up in the everyday tasks of trying to make all their customers and bosses happy and still earn a paycheck. Basically,

---

3   Jim Harter and Annamarie Mann, "The Right Culture: Not Just about Employee Satisfaction," Gallup, January 23, 2021, https://www.gallup.com/workplace/236366/right-culture-not-employee-satisfaction.aspx.

they become disengaged with their job and lose sight of everything. For the most part, Valve+Meter generates nine to ten times more revenue for clients than what we take in ourselves. When you're delivering this kind of return to clients, that's abundance. It's the flow, and it's all the things that come out of an organization growing in a dynamic, healthy way. Everybody we're touching is benefiting.

Although building a strong culture focused on loving, serving, transformation, and accountability is something we have control of internally, we get our best results when clients apply these principles to their own businesses. Obviously, we have little control over a client's internal operations. But what I've found over the past few years is that clients pick up on our strategies and approaches, see the impact they have on their bottom line, and begin making changes in how they operate, which leads to cultural changes as well.

One area where we often see cultural change is with our clients' approach to managing call and answer rates. In the previous chapter, I talked a little about how not answering calls that come in is waste because you lose out on potential revenue. In the call center of one of our clients, there was a culture of thinking that it was okay for an individual to miss a handful of calls on a daily basis. To each person, it's only a few calls they likely don't even realize are costing the company money. But when you look at how it plays out every day across the whole call center and then measure it for a year, it adds up to huge dollars. In fact, in most of the assignments I'm in, it's enough to pay for the marketing that they're asking us to do.

My team had been driving 10 percent of a client's total call volume for a while and saw that they were getting only a 70 percent answer rate. We brought the observation to management and posed that if this was happening in all the call centers, they were losing out on about $200,000 in revenue. The client's leadership said there was no way that was the case and gave all kinds of theories as to why our numbers were wrong. Then the chief operating officer went into their call centers and really dug into the call-and-answer rates right where they were being generated. She found the breakage within the call center culture and, with some changes, was able to get up to a 90 percent answer rate within a few weeks. The company had been suffering some financial stress as a result of the impact of COVID-19, so gaining this kind of revenue boost was a huge win for them. It transformed their financials for the year.

Another part of Valve+Meter's culture that several of my clients have picked up from our coaching is to always build tactics that are repeatable and scalable. When it comes to implementing new programs or achieving growth, many businesses just try ideas they think will work. There isn't a testing methodology or specific, measurable goals. There's no consistent, predictable process for generating growth, which leads to making decisions that are not necessarily replicable into a new market or even a new line of business.

I'm always coaching when communicating with clients, so I use the phrase "repeatable and scalable" often throughout our sales and marketing processes. I want them to organically pick up that idea from me and ask themselves if their tactics are repeatable and scalable. Eventually, I'll hear clients talking about something that's not marketing related—usually something that they're doing in their business generally—and start asking if it will help them repeat and scale. To me, that's a big cultural win.

Sales is usually a place where we can help change the conversations or process. This is particularly true about lead quality and what constitutes a lead. I help set the expectation that the only way you're going to reach your full potential is through repeatable and scalable marketing. That's my responsibility because I'm leading the marketing effort. Sales has to be able to sell the lead coming in and assume that they can close the sale before starting to give reasons why it's not going to close. These conversations often shift a lot between "I'm not getting good leads" or "I'm not getting enough leads." If the data shows that lead quality and volume are correct, the next step is to look to the sales data. Is sales hitting their numbers?

I recently got into this kind of discussion with a client who was upset because we were hitting the targeted ROMS, but the company wasn't growing. When we analyzed the data, we found that his service team had stopped selling. They usually complete two service calls per year for each client, during which there's generally something they're fixing or can upsell while they're in the home. This might not be true 100 percent of the time, but it's a critical revenue stream for profitability. Repair work, tune-ups, missing parts or equipment—there is ample opportunity for revenue at every service call. The data we looked at found that there were no sales tickets for six straight months. Hardly anything was being sold while technicians were on service calls. This was the cause of the revenue collapse, not the marketing. We had an accountability conversation with the client to talk about how the technicians were missing these opportunities. Having the data to show them exactly where their breakage was enabled the client to make changes internally, which shifted the business's path onto one of growth.

To be truly successful, business owners need to be clear about what it is in their heart they're trying to get out into the marketplace.

To be truly successful, business owners need to be clear about what it is in their heart they're trying to get out into the marketplace. Most businesspeople I encounter know what their business objectives are but aren't so clear on the culture piece. The crafting of the culture—the heart part of your business—is missed, and it's a detriment to the organization's growth. You build a healthy culture by being grateful and by investing appropriately in people, wages, benefits, development, and training. It's important to know the stories of the people you work with—clients, vendors, staff—and what brought them to your business. Get to know their names, say thank you, and be aware of what's going on with them. Honor the souls who are walking through your doors every day and trying to contribute to the value of your organization.

You can say that you have great culture, but if you don't interact with people and care about the whole of what's going on with them mentally, physically, socially, emotionally, and financially, you're going to end up with a part of a person in your business, not the whole person. When you have the whole person in a whole job, you have a much more engaged team member who's going to be a healthier worker for you over a longer period of time. This also strengthens your teams to develop and adopt new ways of thinking, such as following the data when developing marketing strategies.

TOOLS FOR GROWTH

VIDEO: JOIN OUR TEAM

Scan the QR code or visit mathbeforemarketing.com/join

MY IDEAS FROM THIS CHAPTER

_____

_____

_____

_____

_____

_____

_____

_____

TOOLS FOR GROWTH

BEST PRACTICE:
HOW TO READ A BOOK
Scan the QR code or visit mathbeforemarketing.com/howtoreadabook

PART 2

MATH BEFORE MARKETING

CHAPTER 4

SIMPLE MATH, BIG RESULTS

M ath was never my favorite subject. I can trace it back to middle school when the baseball/basketball coach was assigned to teach my seventh-grade math class. We would get maybe fifteen minutes of actual instruction. He spent most of the class period talking about practices, games, and other sports-related things because many of his players were in the class. When I started eighth grade, he moved up to coaching eighth grade. This man was my math teacher every year until I was a senior in high school. I learned enough to get great grades in his classes, by his standards, but that wasn't saying much because the teaching was so light. When I graduated high school fifth in my class, I was blissfully unaware of how much damage had been done. When I got to college, I was behind my peers and woefully unprepared for taking college math courses. This deficiency would follow me into the business world.

As you might imagine, I avoided math in college and took only basic courses. I was on a path to become a career librarian, so I didn't think I needed much more in terms of math education. Then, of course, everything changed when I got my first sales job and I shifted my focus to building a professional life in marketing. This is where math would again enter my life and reiterate its importance.

I know, this may sound odd if you are a marketer. So much of marketing is about the creative work involved with developing communications that bring customers to a business. Because of this focus on creative, we lose sight of the fact that there are numbers attached to every marketing effort and decision. Budgets, campaigns, KPIs, ROMS—they're all about dollars and cents, whether you realize it or not. There is always a goal to be achieved, a cost to make it happen, and a need to figure out what kind of profit was made as a result.

This may not be the way you were taught to approach marketing, but understanding the math associated with what we do is essential to making your efforts to achieve transformational growth for your business pay off. Believe me, I know how you are feeling. I went into my education about how the math of marketing delivers huge results with a little kicking and screaming and a good dose of fear. As I started to learn how to calculate costs, growth, returns,

There is always a goal to be achieved, a cost to make it happen, and a need to figure out what kind of profit was made as a result.

and all the other metrics that provide real perspective about the effectiveness of marketing, the more I realized that mastering these concepts would enable me to serve better.

If you are really, truly trying to help people accomplish their objectives, if it's about acting in the long-term best interests of another, and if we're really in these environments to love and serve, then it's incumbent upon us, as leaders anywhere in the business, to get the necessary professional development, to read, to study, and to ask wise people the things we must learn. I was working at Defenders when

I realized that I would need to comprehend the math of marketing very clearly because when I understood the math, and the business and marketing programs grew, we were adding jobs and opportunities.

That really lit me up. I love helping people thrive, get jobs, get promoted, and make a living that they never thought they'd be able to attain. This caused me to dig into the math deeper and to understand how we use marketing to create long-term enterprise value. I owned part of Defenders, and the work I did with the business impacted the stock values. I realized that I was creating abundance not only for the ownership and internal team but also for our vendors and partners. We were buying so much marketing that we needed more supply from our vendors, who in turn had to add more jobs, build more plants, or promote their people. The abundance I helped create extended out to those vendor partners, and that was a really satisfying thing to understand.

One unexpected, but important, effect I found from learning the math of marketing was the ability it gave me to become philanthropic. The growth we had at Defenders allowed us to give in a lot of ways, and I was able to wield a great deal of influence over what those dollars could do. We donated millions that came from a reserve set aside specifically for trying to heal the world with our wealth. In turn, this enabled us to expand our influence. The more I could help others and the stronger my voice got in my business, my community, and the circles I moved in, the more I really understood the importance of this business acumen of marketing math. Ultimately, math landed me in the CEO seat at Defenders and led to the creation of Valve+Meter's vision and mission.

Math before Marketing

At Valve+Meter, we take a math-before-marketing approach to working with every client. This means that we don't implement any actions on behalf of a client without a methodical, data-driven plan. Math, for us, is top of mind in building strategy because it is what helps us define tactics at a particular client's disposal to move their business forward. For us, good marketing results are defined by delivering proven, trackable results using three primary metrics:

- ROMS
- Growth rate
- Profitability

We call our strategy work ThinkFirst. Good marketing strategy starts with understanding the results that marketing must deliver to drive profitable growth and align the marketing strategy with the business strategy. Start with the math before getting attached to the tactics you will use. Employ the data and facts to knit together a robust strategy for financial success and growth.

The following is the basic approach for building a math-before-marketing strategy:

1. Gather the right data needed to set goals and guide decisions.
2. Use the data to formulate hypotheses about tactics that will achieve goals and metrics for determining success.
3. Create a test factory for new campaigns and evaluate the results.
4. Move tactics that achieve target ROMS and that are both scalable and repeatable into the flywheel and increase investments in these working campaigns.

TOOLS FOR GROWTH

CALCULATOR: INVESTMENT & GROWTH RATE ALIGNMENT

Scan the QR code or visit mathbeforemarketing.com/invest

Getting the Right Data

We will spend weeks analyzing the data around a client's business to determine hypotheses, targets, and tactics. Our questions address every portion of the business, from overall revenues and targets to strength, weakness, opportunity, and threat analyses, sales close rates and procedures, operations details, buyer personas, and IT/technical capabilities. Here's a sampling of some of the questions we ask during our ThinkFirst discovery phase:

- What do you want to achieve within the next one to two years?
- What do you want your organization to look like in the next five years?
- What is the annual revenue historically?
- What is the gross margin percentage?
- What is the net profit percentage?
- What is the average revenue per deal?
- What is the overall gross profit margin by line of business?
- What is the lifetime value per customer?
- How many new customers have been acquired annually over the past five years?
- What is the current annual amount of marketing spend, overall and by channel? What has it been each year for the past five years?
- How much revenue is attributable to marketing spend?
- Is ROMS currently being tracked?
- Is there any customer relationship management or marketing automation software in place?
- What is the current sales close rate?
- What is the current call/answer rate, and whom are leads sent to?

The answers to these questions enable us to get a better idea of the landscape the business is working within and provide us with hard data we will use to build formulas and math around programs. We ask questions regarding every part of the business (sales, marketing, operations, and finance); doing so sets an expectation that a holistic approach is what will lead to program success from the beginning.

From there, our team develops a matrix of numbers and KPIs that will guide us as we move forward. ROMS is our most important metric. We look at leads, impressions, likes, followers, organic traffic, number of calls, and what deadlines to hit. But those are leading indicators in the best case and often vanity metrics that tell only part of the story. Without ROMS visibility, you miss opportunities. Some businesses try to measure their marketing value by calculating cost per lead, though even that can be deceiving. Some leads may look really cheap, but they don't convert, or the revenue per deal is too small. Other leads can look expensive, but they convert at high rates and large dollar amounts. The Holy Grail of determining the value of your marketing efforts, budgets, campaigns, or whatever you do under this umbrella is ROMS: "For the dollars I spent on marketing, how many dollars did I get back?"

While ROMS is the ultimate goal, we also want to balance that with growth and profitability. These three things work in tandem in our model. If we're hitting the ROMS but we're not growing the business, or if ROMS is very high but the growth is slow, there is something out of place. There are two things to look at here. You're hitting a working ROMS, so invest more for growth. If you're buying all you can at the high ROMS, assess lowering the ROMS goal to get more market share. For instance, you may want to get a $10:$1 ROMS, but if your competition is spending $5:$1, you will be limited in your marketing tactics, which can lead you to low-converting traffic, generate little to no profit, and compromise your ability to grow. The market is saying that you need to be more aggressive to achieve the ROMS you seek and gain a larger share of the business that's out there for you. The goal is not to hit a high ROMS. The goal is to grow profitably.

When we're thinking about the goal for ROMS, the first thing we do is identify the breakeven point. There are a couple of ways to do this. One simple approach is to divide $1 by your gross margin percent; you will get the minimum number you need to meet or go above your ROMS goal—the breakeven point. Let's say that you want to spend $1 on a marketing activity and you have a 55 percent gross margin. You would calculate your breakeven ROMS as follows:

$$1.00 / .55 = 1.82$$

This shows that when you are bringing in $1.82 for every marketing dollar spent, you've reached your breakeven ROMS and your marketing is not burning cash. This is important when you are testing new things and are trying to see what works, which I discuss later in this chapter. The goal during testing is to find tactics that generate profit without burning cash and that are both repeatable and scalable.

The formula above is assuming all COGS are variable, which is often not the case. A more exact way to calculate your breakeven is to separate all variable costs and calculate the breakeven ROMS to cover your fixed expenses in any given period or by unit produced. To do this for your business use the formulas found in our Tools for Growth

Calculator: Investment & Growth Rate Alignment, by scanning the QR code or visiting mathbeforemarketing.com/invest.

After you've found your breakeven ROMS, it's time to define your goal ROMS. This is the lowest ROMS required to drive profitable growth. Finding this number is counterintuitive to the way most businesses operate. Shouldn't the marketing team be held accountable for the highest ROMS possible? The answer is no. They should be held accountable for getting the most revenue growth without depressing the profit percentage goals. Profitability is the responsibility of all the business leaders, and marketing should be operating in line with the team.

High ROMS is usually a sign of missed opportunities for growth. Take a look at two of my clients who are competitors in the same market. Client A has a goal of $4 ROMS and a 40 percent growth rate. Client B's ROMS goal is $8 and a 5 percent growth rate. Client B is not getting the kind of growth it could because their goal ROMS is too high for the market.

In the residential security business twenty years ago, the ROMS goal of $8 was industry best practice. Today the businesses growing successfully are achieving less than $2 ROMS. And yet I still find many of these businesses with an $8 goal. I know this because they call me about handling their marketing, and I have to say no because the market is too competitive to achieve $8 ROMS.

In businesses where capacity to produce goods or services is an issue, flexing the goals of ROMS is something to consider. For example, ABC sheet metal factory is at peak profit when they are at greater than 85 percent utilization. When it finds itself at 70 percent utilization and labor costs are still being paid, a marketing campaign can get things back to profitability. The factory has a breakeven of $2 ROMS, and the goal of the campaign would be to achieve $5 ROMS. The marketing team could then develop a scalable campaign that shows predictable performance at $3 ROMS. The company can use that campaign to help hit their utilization target of 85 percent and get a strong financial outcome.

My recommendation is to create the ideal business financial model for your set of conditions and then analyze different variables to understand your forecasted results. This will allow you to gain more clarity on how to set your goal. If you exceed that number and what you're doing is both repeatable and scalable, you're growing the business. This is the general math model on which we build ROMS-based marketing plans. However, there is no one set formula for calculating goal ROMS. It all depends on a business's specific needs and goals. I've been using this model for over twenty years, and I still find nuances that impact big outcomes across different industries.

The next set of data you need is a bit trickier to develop. I will go into this in more depth in chapter 5, when I discuss how to buy marketing. To track ROMS, you need to set up systems that can directly tie every dollar spent on marketing to incoming revenue. What does that look like? There is no simple answer to that question. It will depend on your business, the marketing tactics that reach your potential customers and deliver conversions, and the types of tracking that work best with those tactics.

We often establish a revenue tracking system that ties back to dynamic numbers or tags, unique phone numbers and email addresses, and other identifiers. When these items appear in the system, they can be traced to specific tactics we're using, and we see a clear path between the business's data and the incoming revenue. This is just one method for developing good data that builds ROMS calculations.

The last major piece of the data puzzle is getting the right sales information. Sales teams can be reluctant to enter data in many environments. This makes sense because they want to keep selling, not spend time entering numbers into a computer. As a result, they tend to keep their systems easy and simple. However, that doesn't help the business grow and can generate a situation in which bad data is being used to make marketing decisions. The best solution is to automate the leads pipeline in a customer relationship management (CRM) system to prompt sales inputs.

When I talk with clients about measuring results, there are typically four scenarios:

- **No data:** Marketing purchases are made based on gut instincts, past purchases, and industry best practices.
- **Ask the customers:** Call center staff ask the customer how they heard about the business and record it.
- **Bad data:** This is data that is missing information or has incorrect attribution.
- **Good data:** An organized system that captures most data, attributes it correctly, and maintains good data hygiene.

My first choice is for you to use good data, obviously. My second choice would be to not use data at all. Asking customers or using bad data will make you overconfident. I know that it's a common practice to ask the customer how they got to your business or product, and my approach is counterintuitive to what seems logical. The data you get is just not reliable, though. Customers will routinely say that they heard about your business on the radio or searched for you on Google, when the reality is that they've called you from a unique number on a direct mail piece. By saying they found your business from those other channels is misleading. As a result of this information, you will typically buy more marketing than you should and miss some opportunities in which you should be investing.

For example, I used to run ads in the Yellow Pages of every major city in the country. For my younger readers, the Yellow Pages was where everyone looked up phone numbers before there was the internet. You might remember the Yellow Pages as the big book Grandma had you sit on to reach the kitchen table. The ads in the Atlanta Yellow Pages performed very well, and I increased the spend exponentially on this remarkable channel over the course of three years. That was a big mistake.

A new CRM system was put in place to automate the source of revenue generated by the campaign without a human being asked. The result was supposed to eliminate human error in reporting. What happened instead was when customer service representatives (CSR) registered a sale in the system, they got an alphabetized pop-up list of 140 cities to select from. And Atlanta was first on the list.

For three years, the CSRs had been clicking on the top of the pop-up menus and recording sales from all over the country as coming from the Atlanta Yellow Pages. The result was that we wasted $100,000 to $200,000 in spending on Atlanta, but the bigger issue was that those dollars were not assigned to be spent in the right markets. Millions of dollars in opportunity were missed.

Overall, good data is what you want to work with. This is where aligning sales and marketing, then keeping everyone accountable, is extremely important. I've found it to be helpful to count all leads going to a sales team, then measure the close rate across all leads. With some teams I've led, there was often more selling happening between the sales rep and their managers than with the customers. Sales professionals would focus their skills on convincing a manager to remove a lead(s) from the count to reflect a higher close rate. The best closing sales reps were those who were good at having the manager remove leads from their name, not creating sales. The result is bad data, which informs bad marketing decisions and leads to waste. You want to establish and enforce systems that generate good sales data, such as tracking all conversions and leads.

TOOLS FOR GROWTH
CHECKLIST: GETTING THE RIGHT DATA
Scan the QR code or visit mathbeforemarketing.com/rightdata

Working the Data

Once you have the right data, you need to analyze it and look for marketing opportunities. Perhaps the data is showing that conversion rates on digital have slipped and need to be optimized. A new offer you're testing is performing well and should be tested in additional channels. Maybe the majority of your call center leads are coming from a social media ad and not the direct mail campaign you launched a few months ago. Researching social media marketing tactics could be something to look into. Whatever the data shows you, look for areas where you're not seeing great performance and ask what the reasons might be. Then do some more digging to come up with possible answers. Also look at areas that are performing well and ask if there is more you could be getting out of those investments. All of this investigation will help lead you to the ideas and hypotheses you will test out in the next phase of building your marketing math.

In addition to this marketing-specific data, look at information from areas within the whole of the business that may impact marketing. Say you see that close rates or revenue per deal numbers are trailing off. Or maybe the answer rate in the call centers is low (this is a very common problem). Those are numbers to be concerned about because they put downward pressure on ROMS. Marketing can advise the business's leaders about these issues so that they can take advantage of opportunities to improve efficiency. Do you need sales training or more staffing changes in the call center? They can also act on the analysis to cut things that aren't working from a marketing program and invest in things that are, all the while testing for the next opportunities to find campaigns that work.

With the data and analysis in hand, now it's time to act. Cut the campaigns that are not working. Invest in campaigns that are producing results. Plan for your next tests. And most importantly, look for opportunities to increase efficiency and results in the campaigns already achieving the goal. It's often easier to win more in working programs than to find the next new thing.

Taking a math-focused approach also enables us to have tough conversations with our clients when programs are not producing the expected results. If you're going to act in the long-term best interests of your or a client's business, you have to know your data and how to use those facts to show the reality of what's going on in the organization. When I go into new assignments, I consistently find that the data development of the business is mainly focused on operational execution. Operations and finance have concentrated the business's data resources on fulfilling their department needs. It excludes marketing and bars that team from getting the data in a form they need to plan and execute effective programs. This is because it was all designed by operators who view marketing as a cost center and not as a driver of revenue. Or they don't understand what marketing needs for good data.

The Test Factory and Making Decisions

After you've built your metrics for measuring marketing success, evaluated good data, and created several hypotheses for programs or campaigns that you think could lead to growth, it's time to test out your ideas. Your goal as a marketer is to power the flywheel with programs that work by delivering predictable ROMS and cause it to spin faster. You do this by establishing a test factory as part of your math-before-marketing methodology. The test factory is an environment using small, controlled iterations to prove ROMS. The idea is to test small so that you can scale big. A test factory is constantly doing the following:

- Developing strategies/hypotheses for tactics that achieve ROMS
- Testing those ideas based on viability
- Using methodical processes to manage those tests
- Measuring data to develop conclusions about what works
- Determining whether those tactics deliver predictable, scalable results

When a campaign in the test factory is working, you move it to your flywheel to produce repeatable results. Dollars spent in the flywheel are at no risk. They have been proven to work and are monitored consistently to make sure they are still producing. If you can develop a test factory that creates programs that work, then you just keep adding the programs that prove out again and again, making the flywheel go faster while steadily growing the business. That discipline is what's driving this particular model, and you have to stick with this methodology to find the marketing tests that are repeatable and scalable—even when it may seem counterintuitive to what you've learned about marketing.

WHAT TO TEST

Many clients for whom we're building marketing strategy have tried many different things to grow their business. Trying is not the same as testing. When you're trying things without a formal process to engage, execute, and measure, you will burn a lot of cash.

My philosophy is that all ideas are worthy of considering for a test. But before investing time and money into testing in a real-world environment, start with a rigorous internal review to see if it's the right idea to test and what the likelihood is of getting the right outcome. To evaluate whether a tactic is worth testing, ask questions like these:

- What's the math that will make the test work?
- Can I measure it? How will I measure it?
- What are the goals of the campaign?
- What are the forecasted outcomes?

If the answers give you numbers that point to achieving the goals you have, then it may be worth spending some marketing dollars to test this idea. Sometimes you get into looking at these things and find that there isn't enough revenue or number of deals to be helpful. Then you wouldn't move forward investing in a test.

Another thing to consider with any test is whether the program is repeatable and scalable. You don't want to invest in tests that are a one-and-done type of scenario. The real value of a tactic is whether it can be applied to multiple markets, multiple times. I will deprioritize a test if I can make the tactic work in one of my markets but not in any of the twenty others I'm working in. Then I'll refocus my resources on the things most likely to succeed in the least amount of time with the least amount of risk. This approach will also help set into play the order in which we want to start testing things.

When you find an idea worth testing, you have to determine how much marketing you need to buy and for how long you need to buy it to get enough data to see if you're reaching your target ROMS. In some cases, you may need only a few weeks or months for the data to show whether the tactic is effective. In other cases, it could take much longer. It all depends on the business, sales cycles, and other variables that are specific to each campaign.

EVALUATING TEST RESULTS

Test results should fall into one of three categories: failed, winning, and core. If the tactic's data is coming in below the breakeven number, then it has failed and should be cut. You're losing money. A winning result comes in above your breakeven goal. The tactic is generating profit, but there is room for improvement, and it should be evaluated to see what could be done more efficiently to generate more in ROMS. When a tactic hits core results, you have opened a valve. Move the tactic from your test factory into the flywheel and repeat. You also should look at scaling by asking, "Is there more of this we can buy?" This tactic belongs at the core of your growth strategy.

Test Results & Decisions

	STATUS	DESCRIPTION	ACTION
✓	CORE	≥ ROMS Goal	Scale!
✓	WINNING	> Breakeven and < ROMS Goal. Generating Profit Dollars.	Iterate, Re-Test, Improve
✕	FAILED	< Breakeven, Burning Cash.	Cut

Expect that 80 percent of your testing will fail; it's just the nature of effective marketing. You may find that about 20 percent of tested ideas will bring in results above breakeven and that only 10 percent will become part of your core marketing strategy. This investment in testing is essential, though, if you want to build a marketing approach that has as little waste as possible and grows the business. People will ask, "If 80 percent of what I'm testing fails, how will I ever make money?" There's always volume in the things that are working for you at the right ROMS. They carry the smaller tests you're doing in a disciplined, consistent way in your testing strategy.

TOOLS FOR GROWTH
WORKSHEET: MARKETING OPPORTUNITY ASSESSMENT (MOA)
Scan the QR code or visit mathbeforemarketing.com/moa

Math before Marketing in Action

A home services company came to Valve+Meter looking for help growing their business through marketing. They had spent several years building brand recognition for the company through TV and radio ads and had always used a model of budgeting marketing as a percentage of revenue. They were seeing 15 percent growth in revenue annually but thought they could be doing better. My team and I agreed. Based on an analysis of their industry norms, we expected the business to gain 20 percent or more in annual revenues. Here is how we worked with this company to develop marketing math that established a ROMS-based approach and data-driven strategies to achieve transformational growth.

DISCOVERY

During our ThinkFirst strategy work with this client, we found that 75 percent of their current marketing spend was focused on radio and TV top-of-mind advertising campaigns. We found that their digital marketing spend was only 18 percent of their budget when it should have been closer to 50 percent. They had invested tons of money in brand awareness, which had done its job in getting people to recognize the business name. Those budgets increased over time, but the overall growth rate slowed, indicating that the additional spending was not driving growth. When we added in the miss on digital market share, it became clear that this client was losing out on engaging with customers because people could not easily find their company online.

We moved on to analyzing the company's cost to gain new customers. They were spending $294 for each new customer gained in a year. Although $294 is an acceptable number for customer acquisition in this industry, we typically see lower from comparable clients. We also calculated the current ROMS based on the assumption that all growth was from marketing. Those numbers were very low, between $1.90 and $2.60 per dollar spent—and declining. Some of their growth was from acquiring other businesses. If we added in acquisition costs, the ROMS dropped to between $1.55 and $2.29. We would expect to see these numbers landing closer to a range of $6 to $10 for best-in-class ROMS performance.

In addition to this marketing analysis, we also performed a study that looked at the amount of revenue generated per deal made by the sales team as compared to the marketing spend and competitors' performance. Their average deal landed somewhere between $6,800 and $7,500 while competitors were getting deals between $8,000 and $9,000. Although $7,500 was the industry standard for a sale, this company was missing out on much higher figures that competitors were able to get within the same market.

OUR FINDINGS AND STRATEGY

Based on what we learned in the discovery period, we came to the following conclusions:

- Top-of-mind advertising was not helping the company grow. The higher the spend, the lower the ROMS.
- Brand recognition was high, but online visibility was low, despite investments in digital marketing.
- Digital ROMS was already proving to be the highest-performing investment category, but it was still delivering returns below the best-in-class goal we wanted to aim for.
- There was opportunity to increase the amount of each sale, which would also increase ROMS and dominance within the market.

All of these conditions point to stored energy in their flywheel. We recommended reallocating some of the radio and TV budget into digital marketing efforts. As the ROMS numbers grow, they should continue to move money from the media budget into digital marketing that would help people locate their business. We often find our recommendations will not require additional marketing budgets. Instead, we see that repurposing less effective spending into higher ROMS opportunities is often enough to achieve goals.

THE RESULTS

After presenting our findings and strategies, the client decided to keep the same investment in TV and radio advertising but added about $60,000 to the digital marketing budget. We invested that money into a variety of online tactics, such as blog content, e-newsletters, SEO, and paid media, which were the areas where our research had determined were the most likely to deliver the results we were aiming for.

We committed to the client to deliver $1.5 million in revenue at the end of twelve months. After the first six months, we had already generated $1.3 million for this client. Our original target for ROMS was $5:$1. We delivered a return rate of $7.62:$1, and those numbers were rising going into the third quarter. Cost per new customer dropped from $294 to between $106 and $115. Cost per lead also decreased and continued on a downward trajectory as the campaign continued.

Developing the math of marketing just makes sense if you want to turn your marketing business unit into a profit center.

There are so many tools and so much data in today's business world to be used to develop models for measuring marketing. But the approach I created through my work with Defenders and have honed into a model that can be applied to clients who come to Valve+Meter for help growing a business is the most effective I've seen. Developing the math of marketing just makes sense if you want to turn your marketing business unit into a profit center. When you know your marketing dollars are coming back to you in exponential returns, the possibilities for growing your business seem endless. The caveat here is that you not only approach thinking about marketing from a different perspective but also buy and execute your strategies methodically and from that same point of view.

TOOLS FOR GROWTH

FREE: MARKETING ASSESSMENT

Scan the QR code or visit mathbeforemarketing.com/free

MY IDEAS FROM THIS CHAPTER

CHAPTER 5
HOW TO BUY MARKETING

U nderstanding the math-before-marketing methodology is the first part of developing an approach to marketing that delivers transformational results. The next step is reorienting how you buy marketing. Traditional wisdom usually leans toward building a budget based on the previous year's revenues and the upcoming year's sales goals. It's a spending plan that provides a finite bucket of money to invest. A more effective approach is to have an unlimited budget for marketing that works. This doesn't mean that you have an open checkbook, but when you can prove out the ROMS, you should buy all the marketing you can find for that tactic (within the limits of your business's capacity).

Marketing teams tend to lead their annual plans based on what they think will help accomplish their own goals. These can be anything from increasing brand recognition, the number of leads that are funneled to the sales team, customer engagement through digital channels, or responses to specific campaigns. What happens when you take this approach is that you're making decisions about spending money with no real way to track or measure the kind of effectiveness these actions will have on the business's bottom line, let alone return on investment. The instinct is to lead with budgets or tactics, not data-based strategy.

I know an agency that specializes in Google AdWords marketing for large companies and organizations. Their clients' primary goal is to use the million-dollar budgets they've been assigned. The agency never gets an audience with the executives who determine budget amounts. They know dollars are being wasted and are frustrated that they are not in a position to enable these clients to spend more effectively. This budget-focused approach may help the client generate results that may look good on the surface, but it doesn't move the needle toward increased profitability and transformational growth.

Marketers struggle to connect their activities to increases in revenues, yet they rely on vanity metrics to show what their tactics have been able to accomplish, such as numbers of followers on social media. These metrics don't mean much unless you can trace those numbers from specific marketing activities to revenue generated. And you need cooperation and synergy with other teams in the company to accomplish that.

The sales team is responsible for taking the leads and opportunities that marketing generates and turning them into revenue streams. The operations team's job is to implement the delivery of the product or service that the business is providing, field customer questions and issues, and deliver an overall positive experience. The finance team has to pay all the bills and keep money flowing throughout the business. All these teams also work with vendors and have internal responsibilities to maintain efficient systems for manufacturing, administration, and other aspects of the day-to-day tasks needing to be done for the business to work.

Many companies look at finance, marketing, sales, and operations as separate units and do not give attention to them working together as a systemic organization. This approach tends to create a triangle where three of the four essential units are aligned and hitting their goals, but there is an outlier that brings down overall growth and profitability. The result is drag in expanding the business, which is detrimental to everyone involved. For any business to achieve meaningful or transformational growth, all teams must work in tandem and be held accountable to each other.

This is why understanding and adopting the flywheel approach to marketing is vital to transforming marketing from a cost center into a profit center. From there, you can start developing strategic approaches to buying marketing using the math-before-marketing methodology, track data based on real metrics to measure ROMS, and continue to add momentum to the flywheel to get the kind of results that drive growth.

Establish a Flywheel Structure

In chapter 1, I introduced the concept of the flywheel effect from Jim Collins's book *Good to Great*. The general idea is that you put in an initial amount of force to start the wheel rotating. With each rotation, the wheel gains more momentum and releases stored energy, going faster with every turn while you continue to put in the same amount of energy as you did to get things started.

When you apply this idea to a business, the amount of money you spend on marketing to start earning revenue is the initial energy used to put the wheel in motion. The first goal is to discover which tactics create predictable ROMS. Once that happens, the next objective is to continue reinvesting in those tactics, buying as much of the tactic to the point where it achieves the goal ROMS and

Understanding and adopting the flywheel approach to marketing is vital to transforming marketing from a cost center into a profit center.

testing the next tactics with the aim of producing the target ROMS. To move from profitability to a growth stage, you improve the efficiency of the flywheel to where you're getting the maximum possible revenue for each turn while continuing to achieve the target ROMS.

To establish a flywheel structure in a business, you have to view the entirety of the company as a circle comprised of four teams: marketing, sales, operations, and finance. Marketing is the engine for the flywheel. It drives awareness of the company, brand, products, and services; finds prospective customers; and brings them to a purchase decision. It also runs the test factory discussed in chapter 4, which generates proven tactics that deliver ROMS above breakeven.

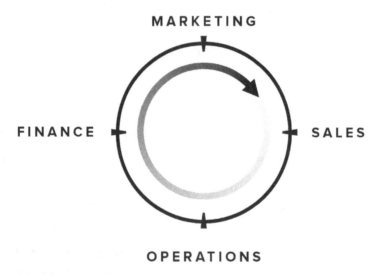

When a new tactic moves from the test factory to the flywheel, the first goal is to optimize it across all business units. Second, you buy all the marketing available for this campaign, then stop when you've bought it all or you're out of capacity in operations. A good rule of thumb for growth is this: marketing never waits on operations. If operations creates a bottleneck, there needs to be pressure to remove the blockage. Stopping and starting working campaigns creates loss of momentum and more energy (dollars) to regain it. A steady stream of programs consistently performing above goal makes the flywheel turn faster each time more proven tactics are added.

Sales comes next. This team is responsible for converting those leads into actual sales revenue and ensuring that each transaction is as large as practical and possible. After the sale is made, the operations team steps up. They provide customer service, installations, deliveries, order fulfillment, manufacturing, and other tasks essential for completing orders and getting customers what they paid for. Finally, there is finance, which is responsible for paying the bills and salaries for the business, spinning off profits, and reinvesting in marketing.

Within this structure, each team in the wheel is dependent on the others to accomplish their goals. When marketing provides sales with the right number of prospective customers enabling their team to convert enough sales to meet or surpass their revenue goals and optimal ROMS, you have a winning formula. When operations is efficient in delivering on customer expectations and sales promises and there is little waste in spending, profits from closed sales increase. And when finance manages costs and pricing effectively, then reinvests profits into marketing that is working to increase revenue, the flywheel becomes more powerful in delivering on its potential and the business is on a pathway to growth.

Managing the Flywheel

When any business unit is underperforming, the flywheel slows down. Similarly, when any unit can improve their results, especially when it can resource marketing more, then the flywheel goes faster. This is why having all four units aligned with each other at a managerial level (at the very least) is so important. It helps identify areas where there may be drag in the flywheel's momentum and opens up conversations about implementing solutions. However, relationships must be cohesive to identify opportunities for growth.

For example, if you bring in marketing programs delivering leads at the right cost and the sales team is not closing them, but operations and finance are doing their part correctly, you form a triangle within the flywheel seen in the following illustration. You can see that there is a big hole in the system, which creates waste and drag. If you were to increase the close rate and possibly the revenue generated per transaction, you fill that gap and the business begins to perform better.

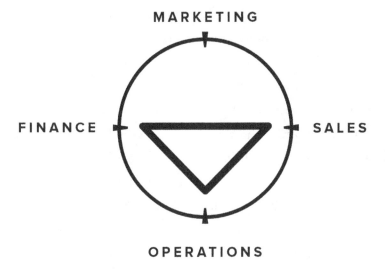

MARKETING

FINANCE

SALES

OPERATIONS

There are four main areas outside of marketing within the flywheel that most often affect my work as a marketer, both good and bad:

- Call/answer rates
- Revenue per transaction
- Sales close rates
- Reputation management

Call/answer rates, in particular, are a common area where improvements can be made. The first step is ensuring that your call centers are being managed to the right expectations. Answering 90 to 95 percent of calls should be standard. Above 95 percent will require too many resources. Fewer than 90 percent means that cash is being lost. Second, the reporting structure should align the call center with the business function it impacts the most. I prefer marketing because the ROMS can be destroyed if calls aren't answered. Sales would be my second choice because not answering calls means that salespeople won't have leads. Many companies bring call center responsibilities into their operations units so that they can streamline sales and customer service. Unfortunately, this tends to result in losing leads because they're not handled properly by those answering the phones, they're not being routed to members of the sales team for conversion, or calls are being missed altogether. When leads are managed by sales, conversion rates are much higher.

The speed with which calls are answered and messages are followed up on can also have a huge impact on the effectiveness of marketing. Valve+Meter conducted a study on lead management and response time in the home services industry. We used a secret shopper to submit lead forms, appointment requests, quote estimates, and other types of inquiries to more than 460 home services companies throughout the US. We tracked response times over the course of five days and researched the kind of tactics they used to generate and track inbound leads. The results were shocking.

- We received a response to only 60 percent of our leads within those five days. This means that 40 percent of our inquiries went unacknowledged or unanswered.
- Ninety-five percent of all companies contacted didn't respond within five minutes.
- Seventy-one percent of them took more than one hour to respond.
- Fifty-five percent of them didn't respond within one day.
- The slowest response time to one of our requests was five days, nineteen hours, and nine minutes.
- Only 37 percent of the companies we contacted attempted to call back via phone; 85 percent of them called us only once in response to our inquiries.[4]

---

4   "The State of Speed to Lead in Home Services," ValveandMeter.com, accessed September 23, 2021, https://marketing.valveandmeter.com/speed-to-lead-home-services.

In the home services industry, the first company to engage with a prospective customer is usually the one who wins the business. The data we generated showed that many companies within this industry are missing out on potential revenue because their call/answer rates are either slow, low, or inconsistent. Marketing is producing the vehicles to bring leads into the funnel, but their revenue potential is being lost. And it's not just revenue. Because you've already paid for the marketing and overhead, the calls/revenue you capture are contribution margin. If you're dropping calls totaling $100,000 in lost revenue and your gross margin is 50 percent, you've lost $50,000 in profit:

> **$100k revenue – $50k cost of goods sold =**
> **$50k gross profit – 0 expenses = $50k profit**

Implementing new practices to shorten response times, adding in more effective CRM tools to track and automate lead responses, and optimizing websites to adhere to best practices are all steps that can be taken to greatly reduce this waste.

The sales team's close rates and the revenue per deal are the big factors that impact the effectiveness of the flywheel, and there's some tension between both of those. If you're closing at a high rate but selling at a low price, your numbers aren't balanced. The salesperson may have great numbers showing that they are making lots of sales but a low revenue per deal. However, they have to work much harder to make the commissions they need to hit goals or earn enough money. On the other hand, they could sell at a higher revenue per deal and reduce their conversion rate. That

The ideal situation is one where you find the right balance of both close rates and revenue generated per deal.

puts them in the same type of situation, where they are performing well in one area but not in the other. Both of these scenarios reduce ROMS.

The ideal situation is one where you find the right balance of both close rates and revenue generated per deal. I recently talked to a business where the average revenue per deal within their industry was $7,500. This company's sales team was getting about $11,000 per deal. With these numbers, I expected to hear that they had a close rate of about 25 percent. But the team was being managed very well by a sales leader who had been hired four years prior when the company was struggling to be profitable. This leader was able to increase their revenue per deal to $3,500 higher than the industry average and achieve a close rate of 60 percent. Those changes have doubled the company's revenue from $6 million to $12 million, with a 151 percent increase in profitability.

While this is a wonderful thing for the company, the sales leader feels they have hit the ceiling with their revenue per deal amount. If they want to continue to grow the business, they would need more leads they can convert into customer sales. When I looked at their marketing unit, I realized that the overperformance of the company's sales leader was masking the underperformance of the marketing team. They only had a part-time person, were not doing well at digital, and were spending most of their budget on top-of-mind awareness programs that were ineffective. Sales, finance, and operations were all doing their jobs well, so it was the marketing part of the flywheel that needed improvement.

The important role the operations team plays in marketing success is too often overlooked, even though it has a big impact. If there are delays in order deliveries or installations, customers cancel orders and revenue drops. There are also issues with having enough staff to keep up with order fulfillment, services, manufacturing, support, and other functions that operations provides. All these factors impact the customer experience, which in turn can have either a positive or a negative effect on how prospects make purchase decisions.

When operations delivers on or exceeds expectations, provides positive experiences, and runs efficiently, customers are happy and help build a good reputation for the business. If customers have a negative impression about a company after having dealt with operations, that makes it harder to convert prospects to new customers through marketing. This is why reputation management is an important area to cultivate within the flywheel. If the customer experience is compromised for a business, word gets around. People tell their friends and family about issues and negative experiences. And with the online world being an essential part of commerce, social media, online marketplace, and Google reviews have become more and more influential in consumer decision-making.

If reviews start to skew more toward the negative and lower scores show up in searches, the business's ability to effectively market online is greatly impacted. If you're not asking for reviews from your customers, getting a good number of recent reviews, and responding to them correctly (such as countering a negative comment with a good customer service response), that impacts business results too. Operations has an opportunity within the customer service space to drive online reviews, monitor them for issues and potentially damaging comments, and optimize them to build positive experiences for current and potential customers.

TOOLS FOR GROWTH

STUDY: THE STATE OF *SPEED TO LEAD* IN HOME SERVICES
Scan the QR code or visit mathbeforemarketing.com/speedtolead

Follow the Math

Once you have a flywheel structure in place, you can start thinking about how to buy marketing. As I discussed in chapter 4, you will use the math-before-marketing methodology to build strategies and tactics proven to deliver on goal ROMS while increasing growth and profitability. The first step is doing the research and data analysis necessary to establish a breakeven goal, ROMS, and other metrics that will be used to measure program success. Next, look for marketing opportunities that could deliver the results you want. Develop hypotheses about how you think a tactic would perform in a real-world environment and evaluate whether you should invest in testing it. Follow the math regarding tactics that consistently test at or above your goal and add them to the flywheel.

This is the basic approach to take before deciding to buy any kind of marketing. You will have all the systems and formulas in place to collect and track performance. Tactics that consistently meet or surpass goals get added into the flywheel and those that can be scaled become part of your core strategy. The more tactics you add, the faster the flywheel spins, so you want to buy as many of those programs as possible. A business with a strong flywheel structure should enable marketing to have an unlimited budget for these kinds of purchases. Evaluating the marketing budgets quarterly rather than annually will allow you to monetize the programs you have launched successfully to accelerate growth and profitability.

While you are buying and running marketing programs that are working, you should also be continually monitoring their performance. Time and circumstances can change how effective a tactic is, which is why you want to have your test factory always developing new ideas that work and make adjustments as needed. Following the math over time will enable you to keep your programs as efficient as possible and move quickly within changing markets.

Additional Marketing Metrics

ROMS is the standard to which most marketing spending should be measured. However, there are other metrics that can be added to your marketing math that may give a more well-rounded picture of how your programs are impacting the business. Here are some you may want to consider.

- **Growth rate:** Subtract the current year's revenue from that of the previous year, then divide by last year's revenue to measure your growth rate. When you pair this number with increased profitability, you see long-term business value. Formula: (Last year's revenue – Current year's revenue) / Last year's revenue

- **Profitability:** When you divide net profit by total revenue, you get a metric that helps assess the health of a business. Profitability increases long-term business value. Formula: Net profit / Revenue

- **Cost of goods sold (COGS):** The total costs directly associated with providing goods or services.

- **Gross profit:** Subtract COGS from total revenue to get this indicator of profitability on services performed or products sold. Formula: Revenue – COGS

- **Gross margin percentage:** Divide gross profit by total revenue to get this important indicator of profitability. Formula: Gross profit / Revenue

- **Overhead or expense:** This is the sum of all expenses not associated with COGS, such as rent, utilities, executive wages, etc. Control of these expenses reduces your breakeven point, so gross profit can create higher profitability.

- **Fixed expenses:** These are total expenses that will not increase when revenue increases. Your fixed expenses should guide decisions about increasing profitability.
- **Net profit:** This is the amount of profit you have after all expenses are subtracted from gross profit. Formula: Gross profit – Expenses
- **Return on marketing spend (ROMS):** This is the amount of revenue that is generated as a result of marketing dollars spent. It proves profitable growth through marketing. Formula: Revenue / Marketing cost
- **Marketing attributable revenue:** This is the total revenue generated and tracked to a specific marketing campaign. You use this in calculating ROMS.
- **Marketing cost:** Total direct cost of a marketing campaign (not including wages, tech, infrastructure, etc.) You use this in calculating ROMS.
- **Goal ROMS:** When your ROMS equals profitable, repeatable, scalable growth, you've achieved goal ROMS.
- **Breakeven ROMS:** To calculate your breakeven point for ROMS, divide $1 by your gross margin percentage. Then aim to stay above that number to avoid burning cash. Formula: $1 / Gross margin %
- **Customer acquisition cost (CAC):** This number calculates how much you spend on marketing to gain new customers. Formula: Marketing spend / Number of new customers
- **Marketing spend as percent of revenue:** This metric should guide growth, planning, goals, and budgets. Divide your total marketing spend by the revenue that is generated. Formula: Total marketing spend / Revenue

- **Answer rates:** This is the number of calls that were answered divided by the number of total calls. As discussed earlier in the chapter, answer rates are a big driver of profit. Formula: Number of calls answered / Number of total calls
- **Close rate:** This is a common measure of success for sales teams and is simply calculated by dividing the number of sales by the number of leads. The rate can reflect lead quality or drag within the sales unit. Formula: Number of sales / Number of leads
- **Revenue per deal/sale:** This is another measure of success for sales teams. Divide the total revenue generated by the number of sales. This average can be influenced by marketing targeting and addressing drag within a sales unit. Formula: Total revenue / Number of sales
- **Lifetime value (LTV):** This is the total number of client purchases made over a period of years. It can be a guideline for how aggressive to be on ROMS.

TOOLS FOR GROWTH

**MATH BEFORE MARKETING
FLASHCARDS**

Scan the QR code or visit mathbeforemarketing.com/flashcards

Track Your Data

As you buy marketing that works, you need to trace those interactions to incoming revenue and measure the success of your spend. There are a lot of ways to trace the path of a marketing action to sales conversions. It starts with tactics that can be tagged or monitored so that when a lead is handed to sales, the source is clear. Google Analytics offers free tools that enable you to create trackable tags for digital marketing activities. You can also set up distinct email addresses or phone numbers that are used exclusively for a specific campaign.

Establishing tracking is only one part of the picture, though. You also need to set up internal data systems following the life of a lead from generation through conversion and into revenue. This is where alignment with all the other teams becomes even more important. If you have leads that are routed to sales and they convert, but the transactions aren't recorded as a result of your campaign, then you don't have accurate data to show ROMS.

Having standard operating procedures to enable lead activity to be tracked from the time it enters the flywheel through revenue generation is vital. Many companies have CRM tools, which can be very helpful in getting systems like this up and running efficiently. However, most CRM programs are set up for the needs of sales or operations, which generates data that differs from what marketing needs. They can be reconfigured to collect all required information and all teams can be retrained on how to use the system. At the very least, every transaction should record a name, phone number, email address, and revenue generation and then attach that data to a category within the business.

Because tracking the right data is imperative for this marketing methodology to work and for you to get the most out of the marketing you buy, I recommend a three-step approach to building a foundation for data capture: organize, systemize, and optimize. Organizing your data points makes for consistency in your business. Systematizing your data points makes information accessible and easily understood. Optimizing from your data points drives your business to efficiency and success.

STEP 1: ORGANIZE

The first step in building a tracking system is to organize your data, and that starts with outlining each business process. To do this, define the outcome of every interaction. Each potential outcome should have its own data point to clearly identify the actions of your business. For example, a business within the home services industry might have several departments, such as HVAC, plumbing, and electrical. They may also have both commercial and residential customers. The types of jobs they perform may include requests for quotes, estimates, warranty sales and services, installations, maintenance or service agreements, etc. Each of these is a data point that needs to be accounted for and able to be assigned to an interaction.

STEP 2: SYSTEMATIZE

To consistently track business outcomes, you need a system. Many businesses use CRM systems that can be customized for their specific needs. If you're adopting a ROMS-based marketing strategy, the most important features for tracking your business include the following:

- **Flexibility and customization:** Look for a CRM that enables you to organize your data the way you need it to be and is flexible enough to mirror your outcomes. You want a system that allows you to create all the data points that are specific to your business (departments, client and job types, notes, etc.).
- **Support and learning resources:** Once you identify a CRM that might fit your needs, get in touch with support and ask for help. Many systems have implementation teams that will help you customize your system exactly as you need it. Take advantage of these resources to save on implementation time and accuracy.

- **Tracking and integration:** The CRM you select must have the ability to report on the information you are feeding into it. Some systems have built-in reporting while others rely on integration to export your data for analysis. Either option can work, but most businesses should start with built-in reporting functionality to uncover and evaluate actionable insights. The implementation team should be able to either set up or guide you in creating customized or even automated reports that fit your needs. Some types of reports you may want to consider include average ticket value per job (broken down by department, client type/job type), average number of jobs per time period sorted by job type, and total revenue by job type.

STEP 3: OPTIMIZE

Use your data to make smarter business decisions. By tracking every job in your system, you will have the insights to identify areas of opportunity, such as the following:

- Do certain job types return higher average revenues?
- Does a member of your team close higher revenues per job?
- Is a specific part of your business doing fewer jobs and less revenue over time?

As you complete more jobs, track more revenue, and analyze more data, you'll be able to answer many more questions about your business and the impact that marketing is having within the flywheel. More importantly, you'll have the actionable data to make marketing buy decisions that drive better results.

Marketing Math and Financial Math

Math-before-marketing thought leadership has some fundamental differences from the way the finance leaders think of math. It's important to understand these differences as you work with financial leadership to adopt these strategies.

Most finance leaders tell me their key frustration with marketing efforts is the lack of ability to measure where results come from. They agree there is an unlimited budget for marketing that works but cannot get the tracking in place either internally or from the vendors delivering marketing programs. When marketing leaders deliver on data-driven results, a powerful alliance with the finance team is created. They help with garnering resources, improving the profit model for the business, holding all business units accountable for the KPIs that affect ROMS, assisting with negotiation, and using a host of other skills.

It is important to remember that there are fundamental differences between finance math and marketing math. Finance works in the world of absolutes and perfection where all the numbers balance. Marketing works in hypothesis, testing, trends, and forecasting where all the numbers are fuzzy. Financial analysis can track every dollar. Marketing analysis, even in the best data environments, is not exact. You're not going to be able to track every dollar generated back to a marketing campaign. Typically 70 to 75 percent can be tracked. Even with millions of dollars of infrastructure on data, I've still only been able to get 85 to 90 percent.

What marketing is looking for in their model is this: Where are we certain enough? If you're measuring ROMS, your number is the worst-case scenario. There is probably additional opportunity in the unknown.

As an example:

- Your ROMS goal is $6.
- You tracked only 70 percent of leads to revenue in your campaign.
- The campaign is coming in at $4.50.
- Breakeven is $2.
- Run it.

Buying marketing looks very different from what you may have learned in college when you have a business with a strong flywheel structure, an abundance of good data, systems optimized for tracking information across all units, and a math-based methodology for developing strategies and deploying tactics. If you're thinking that it might be time to change how your business approaches marketing, there is one more thing to consider: Is it better to refocus or create an internal ROMS-based marketing team, or should you outsource the work to an agency? I'll let you be the judge of that in the next chapter.

TOOLS FOR GROWTH

OFFICE ART: ROMS vs. GROWTH RATE

Scan the QR code or visit mathbeforemarketing.com/art

TOOLS FOR GROWTH

HARVESTING IDEAS

MY IDEAS FROM THIS CHAPTER

CHAPTER 6

BUILD IT OR BUY IT?

When I worked at Defenders, I was a one-person marketing team until the business was about $65 million in revenue. To say that what I did was marketing is a bit of a stretch. I was a businessperson executing strategy and buying marketing. My goal was to drive leads to the sales team, which I couldn't do alone. I outsourced our print advertising to direct mail shops and shared mail providers, and, when the internet became a thing, created online lead generation platforms. The vendors handled all the ad design, printing, mailing lists, and distribution aimed at hitting my target ROMS and brought in a high volume of new business.

When we were about $65 million in revenue, I hired our first two marketing team members. My business role was growing as I took on the leadership of sales and culture, so I needed help managing the vendors and marketing campaigns. As the team grew, most of our hires were managing outsourced programs. For our marketing model—an unlimited budget for marketing that works—outsourcing functioned well. You're engaging the partner in a world built on the agreement to hit the ROMS number, and then I will spend more with you. Over the years, I would say that most of our results were attained through outsourcing.

I was responsible for marketing results, and I focused on only one area within marketing: buying marketing. Today, marketing channels are very prolific. There are so many different specializations that no one person can be an expert at everything. Yet businesses tend to hire generalists to make up their internal teams, then give them the responsibility of managing all aspects of marketing. This places both the team member and the company at a disadvantage because neither has all the tools needed to achieve growth. If you are dependent on one subject matter expert for all or part of your goals, this is high risk. If that person left the company, you have to start over again with a new hire.

Focusing only on the cost of marketing can lead to decisions that generate less impactful results. Traditional business thinking is the smaller the cost, the greater the profit. Cost is relative to results. We may have had less on the books in expenses, but it did not help if we were also seeing less incoming revenue.

Focusing only on the cost of marketing can lead to decisions that generate less impactful results.

So what is the better choice: Build your own internal marketing team, or buy marketing services from an agency that has a whole team of experts contributing to your success? The simple answer is that it depends on your business and what you are trying to achieve through marketing.

In the last two chapters, I've talked about the math of marketing and how to buy marketing so that you're generating profits from your efforts instead of drawing from a finite budget. Similarly, your decisions related to whether to handle marketing internally or externally need to focus on an approach to build measurable, repeatable, scalable, and profitable growth. Will an internal team, an external team, or a combination of both enable you to get all the business that is available in your market and keep things consistently moving forward? Only when you find that answer will you know which choice is right for your business.

When an Internal Marketing Team Is Best

The purpose of your marketing strategy is to achieve financial growth for the business. When people think of marketing in terms of "What do I need to move the needle from here to there?" the natural answer is to hire someone. Whoever the person is, they are going to be a subject matter expert in one or two areas of marketing, not every specialty you need to move the needle. A graphic designer who is skilled at web development might produce a website that looks good but doesn't convert. A web developer who produces a website that converts well may not get the right messaging, content, look, and feel of the website to drive the traffic to even try to convert. To get the results you need, you'll either have to hire a whole team or outsource some, if not all, of your marketing.

For example, if you're trying to drive inbound traffic through your website, you'll need to fill at least five positions: content writer, SEO specialist, web developer, graphic designer, and paid media specialist. Then you need somebody who manages those five people, and all of them must know what to do in order to get the results necessary to win. In addition to this core marketing team, you will also require business development and technical data/infrastructure build-out experts as well as a custom software/technology stack to effectively execute on your digital marketing plans. Even when you have all these positions filled, you've built a team that is optimized only for inbound marketing. If you find that you need to manage the brand, implement direct mail campaigns, TV/radio advertising, billboards, or outbound marketing, you will need additional team members who specialize in those areas.

I see a lot of companies hire someone to handle all their digital marketing. This one person might know a lot about social media and some things about pay per click advertising. But they're not going to be a graphic designer, a website developer, and an SEO expert too. They will lean toward their understanding of the kind of marketing they know rather than take a holistic approach. The idea of testing an array of tactics and then investing where things are working is foreign. In the end, the business doesn't grow because the marketing is ineffective.

To build a team that keeps the business moving forward consistently, you need to start with a marketing leader who works with the other business units to build the kind of strategies and plans that feed the flywheel. They understand marketing methodology based on ROMS and can build plans based on data and measurable results. This enables them to identify what kinds of experts the team needs and allows them to hire accordingly. If the company adopts the practice of an unlimited budget for marketing that works, the leader will be able to fill out the internal team with everyone they need to execute marketing campaigns to achieve a successful return on marketing spend (ROMS) at and above breakeven.

This, of course, is the best-case scenario and can be a sensible approach for some kinds of businesses. There are some trade-offs, though. A well-staffed internal marketing team may be a good option for a large company consistently surpassing the ROMS goal while paying the salaries, benefits, payroll taxes, and other expenses that come with having full-time and part-time staff. With this often comes high turnover and straining the team while you find the right people to replace those who have left and get them up to speed on everything.

Productivity on generating ROMS is also impacted by the internal business needs. Members of this team can be drawn into projects at the request of upper management, have their workflow interrupted by meetings and required professional development, and find it hard to keep up with the latest certifications and best practices because their time and attention is so split between marketing and business needs.

For small or medium-size businesses, the expense may be too great to generate the return needed to grow the organization. In this case, having a marketing leader, manager, and/or as many specialists as it makes financial sense to keep on staff while outsourcing work to an agency may be the right fit to deliver the desired results. The leader and/or manager would oversee the work of the whole team to verify that plans are executed correctly and deliver the right returns and to ensure that everything runs smoothly. Other marketers on the team may work with the agency day to day to accomplish the tasks assigned through the marketing plan.

Businesses best positioned to bring their marketing in-house are sizable and have been working with an agency for some time already. The agency has helped them get their marketing up and running over a period of multiple years. There may come a time when the business considers hiring a content marketer full-time to work with the agency. Then maybe a graphic designer and an SEO specialist. These in-house employees are now closer to the work and can write/design/optimize better than working with an agency for those needs. A good agency will help you add the staff with whom it makes sense to build an internal team, share onboarding and training services, and continue to work with you to ensure that you're setting up your business for success.

If you already have an internal marketing team, you should evaluate the current structure, assess your goals in terms of ROMS and other growth metrics, and determine what skill sets you need to accomplish the growth you want. You may find that your current structure works well. You may also find that restructuring is necessary, you need to add to or reduce your team, or outsourcing some of your marketing needs is the strongest move. Whatever the answers are, let the data and methodology lead your conversations and recommendations.

Key questions to answer before making any decisions about an internal marketing team include the following:

- Is the structure I have for in-house marketing staff consistently delivering on measurable goals that are growing the business?
- Am I currently getting all the results available to me? If not, what can be changed to make that happen?
- How will changes to the team structure help me create a ROMS-based marketing methodology for the business, and what do those changes need to look like?
- Does our leadership know how to manage marketing?

When to Consider Outsourcing

There are several reasons to consider outsourcing some or even all of your marketing. The two most important ones are if the goal you're looking to achieve is greater than your resources and if you don't know how to manage the kind of marketing you need to achieve growth.

GOALS ARE GREATER THAN RESOURCES

There is often a discrepancy between the goals you want to achieve for your business and the resources you need to make that happen. Going back to our earlier discussion about the number of people you need to staff an effective internal marketing team, there is a tendency to underestimate how much and what kinds of resources are necessary to execute on a ROMS-based growth strategy as well as the cost. A leader who is looking to grow by adding outbound marketing might value that program at $300 a week to pay someone part-time to field calls for $15 an hour. That one person can only do so much, and the tech stack, reporting, analytics, and management of the initiative isn't brought into consideration. They're looking at more like a $22-per-hour investment as a base wage and an incentive program based on performance to make this tactic deliver on ROMS. Then they have the added technology, analytics, and management costs. And this position needs a manager.

It's this kind of thinking that leads people to believe that it is less expensive to keep your marketing in-house than to outsource. When you look at the data overall, most of the time you get more of a financial return when you route your dollars to an outsourced marketing team that delivers results based on specific metrics and using a ROMS methodology. It can take three to five years to build an internal marketing team that can deliver the ROMS that an agency can in twelve to eighteen months, during which time you're not moving consistently toward growth. You're investing in your future. And while this can be a good investment to make, you can see growth much sooner if you outsource to a marketing agency with the knowledge, experience, and experts in every area that's important to your business.

A good marketing agency will help you evaluate where your business is at, determine what goals to aim for, and set up realistic expectations about the resources you'll need to grow. The agency already has all the specialists and technology in place to execute a methodical, data-driven plan that will make the best use of resources and get your business on the right track to achieve goals. It also will save you from having to build permanent positions within your internal structure, help you understand the time frame within which you can see ROMS, and frame how it relates to your business's sales cycle.

Additionally, an agency offers a wide array of resources it has already invested in and will use to service your account at a lower cost than you would pay to acquire them yourself. Valve+Meter has developed relationships with technology and software vendors that reduce pricing for building tech stacks and analytics programs. We can use those systems for our clients at a much lower cost because we buy them at a volume discount, but we've also spent the time and money developing them for marketing performance that we know works.

Finally, an agency's staff is more likely to have the highest levels of current certifications and is up to speed with the latest best practices in every area that your marketing plan touches. They are focused solely on providing the services you're paying for without the interruptions that internal teams have. For every project and client with whom they work, agency teams learn more about what is successful and what isn't in all kinds of markets. Then they can apply those experiences to develop stronger hypotheses for testing out of the gate, come up with faster and more effective solutions for a client's needs, and execute more efficiently. All of this saves time, money, and resources while making sure that your marketing dollars are not generating waste.

WHEN YOU DON'T KNOW HOW TO LEAD MARKETING

The other major reason you may want to consider outsourcing is if you don't know how to build or execute on a ROMS-based marketing methodology. You may be a CEO or an owner who has great business acumen. You've been successful in building your business because of your strengths across sales, operations, and finance. But marketing is a completely different challenge for a number of reasons:

- Buying strategies
- Business strategy
- Tactics
- Brand management
- Technology
- Speed of change

For example, there is a specific approach to buying materials and supplies for manufacturing. You get the right-quality products at the best price possible. Then you try to manage that price down as much as you can. In a marketing world, cost is relative to results. If you take this approach to marketing, you're going to find a really cheap product that may not deliver on ROMS. Or it delivers on ROMS but doesn't get you anywhere close to the kind of market share growth that's available to you. Also, when you buy materials, you're not buying all the materials available unless you're trying to create a monopoly. In marketing, your aim is to systematically go after buying up all of what's available to you in your market to get the market share that your competitors can't, while hitting ROMS.

Adopting the mindset and methodology to approach marketing from a ROMS perspective can take a lot of time and patience, especially when you've subscribed to traditional thinking your whole career. This can lead to barriers in implementing marketing effectively. You have to understand that marketing initiatives take longer to deliver results than you'll typically see with sales, operations, or finance. This is especially true in the business-to-business (B2B) space, where the sales cycles are long. We may start a marketing project today for a B2B company, but it may take twelve to eighteen months from the time the leads come in to make it through the sales cycle and generate actual revenue. Then add another six months to get consistent data and analysis. It takes a lot more patience than what most CEOs are used to, and that's often where I see businesses go off track. They want immediate gratification.

Working with an agency can help bring business leaders into the ROMS-based marketing headspace without having to fully learn all the intricacies of practicing the methodology. We work as part of the existing team to do what we do best: produce and execute repeatable, scalable, and profitable strategies to grow businesses. We set expectations, provide plans that are mutually agreed upon, move forward with testing and tactics, then provide regular data as to how the work is producing ROMS. We also help keep you on track when the desire to make changes outside the scope of the plan arises.

One of the first things that often happens with a new client is that the CEO or the marketing manager wants us to do something different from the agreed-upon strategy, thus shifting the entire construct of the plan we agreed upon. This comes from more traditional ideas around what marketing should be, information about what competitors are doing, gut-based desires for what they want to see, etc. When I hear this, I explain that I can do what they want but that it will blow up ROMS altogether because I don't know what the new tactic will yield. Then I can't deliver the ROMS originally promised. The issue isn't that it's a bad idea. It's that implementing it is a departure from the strategy, and it's my job to keep the client on track based on the data we know. If we say that we will do it, then it is done outside of our core work in a time and materials test that doesn't contribute to ROMS. Test! Test! Test!

Many of my clients receive advertising dollars from manufacturers, franchisors, or other partnerships that must be used for specific types of marketing channels. Often these approved channels are not ones that will generate results for the client. For example, one of my clients was successfully growing their business and profits through a group of tactics, achieving $8:$1 ROMS. They got $80,000 from a manufacturer to spend on marketing. The list of approved channels was very weak for this client's market and included direct mail, shared mail, and some paid social media options. By themselves, these are not bad marketing channels. But for this set of client conditions, they were not good choices for investing marketing dollars.

My team measured what the ROMS would be if we spent this money in the approved marketing channels and got a $0.50:$1 figure. At first blush, you might think that's not such a big deal because it was free money from the manufacturer. The client wouldn't lose any money by investing it in the approved channels. That's not true, though. When ROMS are below breakeven, it costs the company to run those campaigns. That $80,000 spend created $38,400 in revenue. Their breakeven was $2.50 ROMS. So they actually burned $40,000 ($120,000 – $80,000 co-op). If that money had been spent on the things we already knew were working, it could've generated $640,000 of revenue.

This desire to lead marketing with the gut, according to the guidelines of others, or to follow the latest trend is so strong that having an agency to reel you back into the plans that have the highest potential to deliver growth ends up saving so much in resources. You shouldn't take on ROMS-based marketing on your own until you really understand how it works. You have to be able to measure it, achieve it, and know what to do with it when it is working. Most business leaders and CEOs are not in this position, and it leads to waste in marketing spend and efforts. If you simply must have all of your marketing as an internal unit, then work

> *You shouldn't take on ROMS-based marketing on your own until you really understand how it works.*

with an agency to learn this approach and get your team set up so that they will be able to deliver on the growth you want. This will enable you to invest in your in-house structure while you grow in the short term and set your organization up for long-term success.

TOOLS FOR GROWTH

FREE: MARKETING ASSESSMENT

Scan the QR code or visit mathbeforemarketing.com/free

How to Work with a Marketing Agency

When you choose to work with a marketing agency, or any vendor for that matter, you should approach the relationship like they are an extension of your internal team. If you hire someone new within your business, they will need time to onboard, train, and find their stride within the company structure. You want to be transparent with a new hire and help them grow into their position so that they can provide the most value possible. The same is true when you work with a marketing agency. Be open and candid with them about your goals, long-term vision, expectations, and resources. Give them time to learn about your business and how it works so that they can execute the right plans for your growth.

I've seen clients who view the vendor relationship as something almost adversarial. There is a tendency to believe that an agency will try to screw you out of your money while delivering very little in results. If you're working with a good agency or vendor, this is far from the truth. A good agency, like a good employee, understands that adding value keeps you in the job. But it's understandable to feel that way if you've been burned in the past. Just don't let those experiences guide how you work with vendors in the future. The key is offering trust but verifying that you're getting what was agreed upon from the vendor. Only work with agencies that are transparent with their data and give regular updates as to how plans are being executed as well as what results are being seen.

It's also important to set realistic expectations about when you'll see results. Allow thirty days for onboarding and ninety days for the agency to get a handle on everything that's going on. It will take at least six months before you're seeing great results. The longer the sales cycle, the more time it takes to see revenue. You would allow that much time for a new hire to show how they will perform in their job. You should do the same thing with a vendor if you're going to get the most out of the relationship. A good agency will set up timelines and regular reporting so that you can see exactly what is being done and whether you're on track for achieving the goals you want.

Finally, and most importantly, you want to get to know the people and company you choose to work with. Our goal is to love, serve, and transform. This extends to the client/vendor relationship because when you approach working with vendors from this perspective, you generate results that benefit everyone and get the best performance from all involved. When I was at Defenders, I took the time to get to know the vendors I worked with, what their goals were, and what was important to them. I openly shared what our goals were and told them that I had an unlimited budget to buy marketing from them. All I needed to know is if it was successful and then I would buy all of it I could. It was a big motivator for the vendors I worked with. It caused them to look for the right solutions for my business and bound them together with me in a partnership to hit a ROMS.

When I did that, vendors came to their meetings prepared to show results. They were excited for me to share my results and to think through how we could do more of this. When we found things that didn't work, we thought through what was needed to get to the goal and what our next opportunities were for expanding what we did with them. Some vendors developed new products and services to help me win. Some ended up cutting their prices significantly to get me to go to a nationwide footprint. Some helped me with extra data analysis and tools. And some vendors charged me more for premium placement or exclusivity that lifted my results dramatically.

For example, Valpak put some of the top data analysts available in the country at the time onto analyzing what was working for me in their program. They helped find where cuts and increases should be made. Their president, Jim Sampey, helped us personally. That's the kind of collaborative experience you get out of internal team members who work for your company, and it's the kind of relationship you should have with your marketing vendors. When you're focused on those things, you're giving them feedback on what's working well and what's not. These become candid conversations very similar to employee performance reviews. You collaboratively share goals and results, hold the vendor accountable, and vice versa. This is exactly what you do with your internal team members and what you should be doing to build a profitable relationship with your vendors.

A few things to be wary of with agencies:

- Always make sure you own your website.
- Be cautious when it's really cheap.
- Ensure that you will have access to your data.
- Test small and scale.
- Hire an agency willing to stop doing what is not working and do more of what is.

Over the last three chapters, I have shared a lot of advice and information challenging much of what you know about marketing and business. But for more than twenty years, I have seen this approach generate millions and millions of dollars in growth. It transformed companies in ways their leaders never dared to dream about. And when you achieve that kind of financial growth, you are also growing personally. You're developing an abundance of business acumen and strengthening your skills, which puts you in a position to continue growing and to share what you've learned and earned with others. So with all this growth, we need to be attentive to developing leaders. This is where the journey gets fun.

MY IDEAS FROM THIS CHAPTER

PART 3
_____

ABUNDANCE

CHAPTER 7

BEAUTIFUL BY GOD'S DESIGN

For we are God's masterpiece. He has created us anew in Christ Jesus, so we can do good things he planned for us long ago.

—EPHESIANS 2:10 (NLT)

I recently chatted with someone in a business group about the idea of success. When he was young, he was a really good swimmer. But he had a coach who told him he would never amount to anything. That boy carried those words with him into adulthood and the conversation we were having. He told me that if he didn't get his company to $10 million in revenue, then he will have failed as a businessperson. He repeated this over and over during our conversation, showing how important it was for him to reach this specific number. It turns out that he had set this goal of $10 million in his mind many years ago as a benchmark of achieving success and making something of himself. When he reaches that point, he plans to write a letter to his old coach to show him how wrong he was back then.

The truth was that he could've written that letter the next day because he was already good enough. All of us are perfectly created. We are all unique, and we all have something that's trying to get out of us and into this world to add value. We are all loved beyond measure by God, and we have this access to him through Christ that is just beautiful in a healthy Christian relationship. Yet, somewhere in childhood, we become wired with this message that we aren't good enough. We don't have what it takes. We are missing something and just don't measure up.

All these messages play in our heads as children, even in the best of parenting environments. As adults, these thoughts continue to guide our feelings about ourselves, influence our actions, and often hold us back from reaching for the things we can achieve. We feel like we have to impress other people or be liked by everyone. Sometimes it's having the things that represent success—a home, a car, a beautiful spouse, perfect children, a title, or however else we define success. What it can take a lifetime to realize, though, is that none of it matters.

I came from a rough upbringing and a broken environment. I was constantly getting input from family, kids at school, teachers, and others in my world that I simply was not good enough. I learned that the way you prove you're good enough is to get straight As, win awards, earn ribbons, be in athletics—all those things in childhood that provide some tangible measure of your worth to others. It wasn't until I was well into my forties that I began to realize that I am perfect just as God made me.

The day I lost just about everything and found myself on my knees crying in my living room and holding my babies changed everything. I was able to quiet my mind long enough to hear what God had been trying to tell me all my life. I am strong. I am capable. And I have all the tools I will ever need to do the work he put me on this planet to accomplish. I just needed to accept God's path for my life and become the best version of myself so that I can use that wisdom and abundance to raise my boys into men and serve others.

It took my entire adult life to pull back the layers enough to finally see that this was the way forward. Today, my life is extremely joyful. I'm not tethered by all the things people say (good or bad), and I am fulfilling what I was created to be. I am in a place where joy, effectiveness, and abundance happen not only for me but also for the things I'm working on and partnering in. If I go off that path, then it's not an anointed path and I don't get any fruit from it.

In this final section of the book, I want to share with you what I've learned about how to transform oneself, others, businesses, and the world so that you can reach this same place of joy much sooner than I did. I want to help you find a space where you can become centered and push down all of the voices and doubts in your mind about your own potential and abilities. More than anything, I want to help you unlock your full potential so that you can share that abundance with others and make an impact that can change the world. This is important to master because the things you've learned so far will grow your business. You will need to grow too. The first step is to look within yourself.

Change Begins Inside

I firmly believe that all meaningful change starts on the inside and works its way out. It takes time and a conscious effort to look within yourself to find the things that may be holding you back and then address them in a healthy way. You've made agreements with yourself about what you expect and what you will accept in your life.

For many people, those ideas are hinged to the way you were brought up as a kid and not based in reality. They're often built on things other people told you in school (kids, teachers, bullies), in broken relationships, and in toxic situations. And maybe—probably— life's little mistakes or big failures have created fear or confidence issues. As a result, you may have accepted those things as truth when they were not. Identifying what those beliefs are and breaking them apart is what enables you to free yourself from these false agreements you made with yourself early in life.

I find myself doing this kind of work all the time. If I feel anxious, I stop and ask myself, "What is this thing I'm experiencing?" The answers are all the same. I'm fearing I'm not going to do this or that and I'm ashamed of it. I'm going to miss a goal and I'm going to look bad. My reputation is going to be hurt when somebody says something about me missing that goal. I run into thoughts like this all the time.

I think women, especially, are conscious of when somebody talks badly about them. We spend days ruminating about what he/she/they said, going over the hows and whys and what could've been done differently. I've learned that it just doesn't matter and that you have to let it roll off your back. The people who will speak badly about you or try to tear you down are broken. You don't have the time or energy to try to fix them, nor should you. Your job is to get clear on what it is you're here to do and then spend your time and headspace in those spots.

Focus on Strengths, Not Perfection

One of the most powerful pieces of advice I've ever heard came from a series of CDs by Jim Rohn. They were given to me as part of a seminar about living a successful life, and I would listen to them during my three-hour commute when I worked at Defenders. The topic was how to build your best life, and the quote was this: "Learn to work harder on yourself than you do on your job. If you work hard on your job, you can make a living, but if you work on yourself, you'll make a fortune."

That simple statement went through me like a knife. It encapsulated what happened to me when I got up off my knees in my living room and decided I was done with failing and was going to start learning something every single day. It was how I have been living my life ever since. What surprised me was that Dave had been listening to the CDs at the same time and the same quote stood out to him too. He called me about five minutes after I had heard the same quote. This was decades before podcasts were a thing. We both saw getting everyone at Defenders to understand this concept was the best way the company would grow. When your people are growing and progressing personally, then your business grows as well.

This was the ultimate confirmation that my approach to life was the right one to take in business. When I'm working with people and helping them achieve transformational results, I don't need them to get all the things done that are placed in front of them. What I do need them to do is get the most important things done and continually be developing themselves so that they can keep pace with the growing business. Most people and business leaders don't understand that they don't have to be perfect, nor do the people they lead. It's okay to fail. It's okay to learn. It's okay to be wrong. The number one enemy of success for people can be perfectionism—something that just doesn't exist.

When your people are growing and progressing personally, then your business grows as well.

The idea that we must do things perfectly creates a lot of downward pressure on your ability to perform in a healthy way. It's important to understand that failure is not a weakness. There are going to be times when the things you try are not going to work out. If you hold this model of perfectionism up to yourself, you're going to create a lot of stress. Accept the failures and learn from them. Appreciate what you become in the failure and then carry that experience forward to win in the future. That is how you grow.

Getting results is not the same as being perfect. Often, you'll have a project that has maybe ten steps to it. After finishing eight of the steps, you get the result that the project was created to do. Do you really need to accomplish those last two steps? I see people become mired down in projects. They'll get it to 95 percent in the first three weeks but then it stays at 95 percent for the next three months because this one thing is not done. But the project is getting the result that we created it for to begin with. Yet people will drive themselves nuts feeling they have to check all the boxes and completely miss the fact that getting things done is better than doing something perfectly.

I find myself spending a lot of time coaching and mentoring people and pulling them off this idea of perfectionism. I lead them toward discovering their strengths and understanding that they don't have to be good at everything. God has made us all in unique ways. The idea is that I'm bringing something to the world that's different from what you are. Understanding what your strengths are and spending time in those areas is important. You can discover what those strengths are through any number of assessments, but that's just a jumping-off point.

Spend your time understanding how you're wired. Observe yourself doing things well. Observe yourself in your work, on what is bringing life and energy to you and what is draining it. If you're working on something and you lose track of time, space, and people, and you're really enjoying that work, that gives you an idea of where those strengths are at. If you're constantly doing things that drain you, that's probably because you're bumping up against weaknesses and things you're not really wired to do.

The key is to identify and manage those weaknesses and spend energy on making your strengths even stronger. Create defense mechanisms through your weaknesses, like systems and processes or surrounding yourself with people who are good at the things you're not. This enables you to tap into mechanisms when needed so that you can do what you're built for in your strength zone.

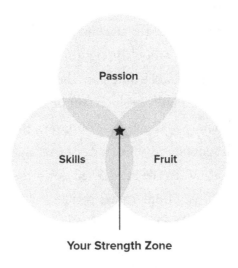

The space where your passions, your skills, and what you can get paid for (economic drivers) intersect is your strength zone. It's great to be passionate about something, but if you can't get paid for it, it's not going to be your career. If you're passionate about something and you could get paid for it, but you're not good at it, or you don't have the skills yet to do it, you're not going to build a career here. Focus your energies in the middle of where these things intersect.

Be a Conqueror, Not a Victim

One of the most important lessons I took from the way that I was brought up and the journey I've taken throughout my life is that it is much more effective to be a conqueror than a victim. There have been plenty of times when I have stepped into that victim role, not the least of which was during my childhood when a boy who lived just up the road bullied me every day from the time I was in the first grade until high school. He was a few years older and for some reason took every opportunity he could to beat up on me and my younger sister, Julie. I was a smart, quick-witted kid and could slay him verbally whenever he would try sparring with words. I think he found it much easier just to punch me because he had the size and strength advantage.

On the first day of school in eighth grade, I got on the bus hoping that this year would be different. The boy would always sit at the back of the bus and bully everyone on board. But now he was a high school sophomore who may have outgrown the need to do this, I hoped. When he got on the bus that day, he sat right in front of me, which was unusual. When the bus started down the road, he turned around and said, "If you think things will be any different this year, you are dead wrong." Then he punched me in the nose while the bus driver watched the whole exchange in the rearview mirror. My new white shirt was covered in blood, and not one teacher asked me that day what happened.

When I got home, my mother was furious. For years she had routinely taken us to this boy's house demanding justice from the mom when he would smash an orange on my head, beat up on Julie, steal our money, or whatever else he did to abuse us. Justice never came until that day. Mom piled us all in the car to go to our local store and buy our first pair of high heels. Our clothing budget was gone, and we probably went without something to afford three new pairs of shoes. But we were able to pick out the ones we liked best under Mom's guidance, "so long as they had very high heels." Back home, mom showed us how to use our heels as weapons to defend ourselves. She coached us, "He can beat up one of you, but he can't take all three of you at the same time." We wore our heels the rest of the night to get used to the feel of them, pretending we were Charlie's Angels while we karate chopped and roundhouse kicked through our chores.

The next day, my sisters and I got a lot of attention in school, and we felt powerful being the first ones to wear high heels. On the way home, the boy up the road didn't bother with us until we were about ten minutes from our stop. He decided to start hitting Julie. Nancy, my youngest sister, and I joined in, and the three of us jumped this kid while the bus was still moving. We punched, kicked, scratched, and bruised him until the bus driver did something he had never done in the eight years we were being beaten. He stopped the bus and pulled us off the boy. Then he started yelling at us. "What is wrong with you girls? Have you lost your minds? Why are you beating up on that boy?"

We sat in the front seat until the bus reached our stop. Mom was at the end of our driveway waiting for us, which was both scary and unusual. She had a habit of telling us to do something and then getting mad when we did it. We thought we might be in trouble for beating up the boy. As I looked down the road, I saw my mom sitting on the hood of our big yellow station wagon. The sun was shining on her hair, and she was smoking a cigarette. I don't know if I ever saw her look more beautiful. When we got off, the bus driver exasperatedly told her what happened. Mom told him that's the way it was going to be until the boy learned to keep his hands to himself. Then she flipped her cigarette to the ground and walked away.

Not twenty minutes later, the boy and his mother knocked on our door looking for justice, just like we had so many times before. Mom said he had it coming, and her girls would keep fighting back whenever they needed to. I'm pretty sure that boy got a beating at home that night, not because he had hit us but because he had been beaten up by girls. He never touched us again.

My mom was not an easy woman. She was rough with us girls, but she was not going to allow anybody else to be. In that moment, she taught us that we had value, how to defend ourselves and be independent, and how to handle a bully. I've carried that programming with me throughout my life and have called on it a lot during my career and in my personal relationships. When I encounter people who want to do business with me but show up with that attitude, I simply say no, I'm not going to do it because I'm more valuable than that. God has better plans for me. Why would I help somebody with that mentality to create abundance in their business anyway? Would it even be possible? It's just not the space I'm called to.

It's a much stronger space to be in when you're confident in your worth, abilities, and purpose. You're a conqueror now and won't become a victim unless you allow someone to take that confidence from you. I've done a good job of ingraining that in myself, so much so that I can walk into a room without even speaking and have authority. I would have never thought that would happen to me. But it's the internalization of my Father's creation in me that's emanating into the world.

Sometimes I think we mistranslate the feelings or thoughts we have in moments of stress. When you're in a confrontation, you might feel that you deserve the treatment you receive. This is when you have to pause and assess what is going on. Ask yourself if you're really wrong or out of line. Is this something you really need to give credence to or hear? Is this constructive criticism, maybe even in the form of shouting, or is it bullshit? Figuring out where that tension lies and getting good at discerning it is a skill that is irreplaceable in anything—business, raising children, leading groups, and personal relationships.

I recently got into a business situation with a bully. My team was delivering strategy to a client who began bullying all of us within five minutes of the start of our presentation. I intervened and tried to be graceful while holding my authority. The man knew the value of my team and the experience I brought to the table. He was in his sixties and getting ready to hand over his $16 million business to his son, which is understandably stressful. But after trying to defuse this tense situation for about seventy minutes, I had to stop the meeting.

An earlier version of myself would have said that I probably deserve what this client is giving me. It's okay if he bullies me because I can handle the stress. But I'm very aware that my team can't. The body reacts when somebody bullies you. The brain releases cortisol, which fogs your mind. So now you're not able to do your best strategic thinking, presenting, or communication. All of that gets blurry. When you see somebody else being bullied, the physical response is worse. That's the empathetic nature of the human condition.

When my team saw me get pushed by the client in the first five minutes of the meeting, they were making mistakes in their delivery throughout the presentation because the situation impaired their brains from working the way they should. Another leader might have blamed the team for giving a bad presentation. That was not the case. I knew it and named it for what it was. So I stood up for my team because they did the best they could under the conditions that were forced upon them.

I am not a toxic leader, and that means I will not bring toxic relationships into my business and expect my teams to deal with the fallout. Beyond this being a moral imperative for me, it results in turnover from the stress and pain caused by these relationships.

My team saw all of this unfold before their eyes and thanked me for standing up for them. One of the team members, a woman in her late twenties, said, "I've never seen another woman, or a man for that matter, step up like that and just be point-blank candid with the truth. It really gave me a very good view of what good looks like." That young woman will take this experience with her, and it will strengthen her throughout the rest of her career. She will be a conqueror, not a victim.

Break through Ceilings

As you go along developing yourself, there will be times when you hit a ceiling. This has happened to me several times in my career. I would reach a spot where I just couldn't get to that next level. You'll encounter times when you're bumping against this invisible space and it is preventing you from taking the next step forward. I'm not talking about the proverbial glass ceiling but other barriers that may be holding you back, such as experience, knowledge, confidence, fear, etc. When you find yourself in such a position, you have to look beyond the ceiling itself and figure out what you need to do to break through that barrier.

Start with assessing your strengths and honing the ones that will help you move forward. Then become an expert on the ceiling. A common practice I used was that if there was something I needed to master, I just went deep on it. I might pick up three books on a topic to start to get some expertise on it. Then I would read three more books and keep going until I gained enough knowledge to be fluent on the topic. Next, talk to other experts and keep learning. Get perspective from them on how to get through that ceiling. Who has bumped up against this before and knows how to break through? What can you learn from them?

The next stage is to engage with good coaches and put what you've learned into practice. I was the director of marketing in a company with deep financial skills, and the ceiling I was facing was math. As you know from chapter 4, math is not my favorite subject, but I knew it was imperative to master for me to move forward in my career. During that time, everybody around me was using a new tool called Excel for their analyses. I didn't know this program well, so I relied on others to run data for me. This was part of my ceiling because Excel was the vehicle for the math I needed to learn.

When I was out of work for six weeks after breaking my leg and undergoing surgery, I chose to complete a bunch of Excel tutorials online while I recovered. I practiced with our business data and discovered some opportunities we had not seen before. When I came back, everyone was shocked that I had learned Excel, and they were pleased to capture the findings in the data. This didn't break through the ceiling, but it got me one step closer to achieving that goal.

After you've learned about your ceiling, been coached on it, and done some practicing, you can really seal the expertise you need to break the barrier by teaching others. This is the ultimate way of learning something because what happens is so joyful. Not only do you break through the ceiling but also you grab a few other people and you pull them through that same ceiling with you. They may not have even known they had hit a ceiling yet, but you've just given them the tools they need to smash it completely. And that's a wonderful feeling.

Deal with Curveballs

Lost jobs, failed relationships, health crises, pandemics … these are just a few of the curveballs you'll have to deal with in life. Good or bad, I've experienced so many curveballs that I've developed a process to get through them. When you have a process, especially a written process, to handle a curveball, you are less likely to be caught off guard and more confident that you can and will get through it. And sometimes the curveballs are *huge*. Maybe even a knuckleball. In the words of Jimmy Cannon, "A knuckleball is a curveball that doesn't give a damn."

You can face curveballs or the more drastic knuckleballs using a similar approach to breaking through ceilings. Some of this is going to fly in the face of our natural reaction. But I can tell you, when you're staring one of these curveballs in the face, the first space you need to get yourself into mentally is gratitude. Be thankful for the curveball and what you'll become as a result of its impact. Be thankful for the experiences you've had in the past that will help you get through the situation. Look around you and assess all the things you have to be grateful for. Get into journaling and write down five things every day that you're thankful for, because when you can get in that mindset of gratitude, it'll frame you up to be a conqueror and not a victim. That's a very important first step.

In 2017, I was diagnosed with Parkinson's disease. I sat in my car after that appointment and cried for about twenty minutes. Then I started praying through this curveball. It became very clear to me that I had spent over twenty years telling my son Ryan that his cerebral palsy did not hold him back from helping others and making an impact on the world. I was so grateful that those twenty years had built muscles that I would find useful in my own circumstance. I would meet new people and encourage others. At the end of those twenty minutes, I said, "Well, God, let's see what you do with this!" I put my car in drive and moved on down the road.

After you've found your gratitude, take an inventory of all the experiences you've had in the past that can help you get through this curveball. We often sit in these spaces and think it's new. But is it really new to you? Is there something else in your experience set that can help you there? Do you have friends, colleagues, business associates, or resources that can help you get through this curveball? Take a moment to ask yourself, "Where do I need to go? Who do I need to talk to? What do I know about overcoming this?" Once you have your answers, talk to experts who have gotten through a similar space in life as well. Look for wisdom that will help you move forward. The thing you don't want to do with a curveball is just hold it. Find a coach who will help you learn how to do this and guide you through the process as you learn.

The last two steps for dealing with a curveball are to serve and give. Ask yourself, "Who can I help?" In serving, you are helping to gain a greater understanding of how to find joy and even comfort within the situation, thereby helping yourself move forward through the curveball. Shifting your focus from self to others is powerful. Ryan's cerebral palsy was a huge knuckleball for me. As we worked through it, I evolved into a better parent for both of my children. I received formal training and became an advocate for adults and children with developmental disabilities. I helped other parents negotiate education plans for their children. I got involved in philanthropy connected to this area. I've done a lot in the more than thirty years I've been in this space, which has allowed me to be a better servant to other people, and I get so much joy from that.

Many times our curveballs are financial. I lost my job. I'm getting a divorce. I've got this problem with a child. Something financially is giving me pressure. Even when it's a financial thing you're dealing with, look for opportunities where you can give to others. I find that when I *give* in a curveball, I release attachment to money or things and trust God to do his thing. In God's economy, you can't out-give him. So when you're going through the curveballs, pay particular attention to whether you're giving and being a good steward of the resources in front of you. Because it is mind blowing the things that have happened to me when I *give* in the curveball.

The COVID-19 pandemic was probably the biggest curveball of my life. I really thought there was a good chance at the front end that I was going to take a huge hit, maybe fail financially from all the things that were changing in the world and with my clients. It was so overwhelming that it took me a couple of days to get back into my own process and find a way through using the same advice that I give others. I started with giving my stimulus check to a ministry that was financially helping missionaries from Mexico through the crisis. I spoke with other people I know and convinced them to do the same. Within a few days, we raised thousands of dollars for that ministry. That brought joy into a dark time because not only was I giving but also I was influencing others to do so.

By addressing the messages and ideas that are holding you back from achieving your potential, you increase your ability to grow.

Then I thought this was a good opportunity to get my team at Valve+Meter involved in giving. We started a campaign for a local homeless program in Indianapolis where the company would match any dollars donated by the staff. They gave $2,500 of their own money and I matched it through the company, so we made a $5,000 donation to help keep homeless families together. The night I announced the campaign to my team, I received approval for the Paycheck Protection Program loan I had applied for from the CARES Act. It was approved for more than I requested. The difference between what I asked for and what I received was almost exactly the amount of the stimulus check I donated to the ministry and Valve+Meter's matching donation for the homeless. We will come back to giving later.

Why is all this important? Why should you work on becoming a stronger and more developed version of yourself? Because you've been created for something special. You're on a mission. There's something here that you're trying to do that's important to our world. By addressing the messages and ideas that are holding you back from achieving your potential, you increase your ability to grow. As you grow, you are able to heal and become stronger. A stronger you has influence to heal and strengthen others, which then multiplies to heal the world as a result. It's important to not get discouraged and instead to keep on growing. We've got big, big plans for you to be able to do better.

TOOLS FOR GROWTH
WORKSHEET: CEILINGS & CURVEBALLS
Scan the QR code or visit mathbeforemarketing.com/breakthrough

MY IDEAS FROM THIS CHAPTER

CHAPTER 8

TRANSFORMATIVE LEADERSHIP

Do nothing out of selfish ambition or vain conceit. Rather,
in humility value others above yourselves, not looking to your
own interests but each of you to the interests of the others.

—PHILIPPIANS 2:3–4 (NIV)

Throughout this book, I have shared what I know about growing a business in a significant, transformational way. You've learned about marketing math and new ways of thinking. I spent a lot of time talking about business acumen and developing yourself to be both strong and strategic. These are the building blocks for creating a career and/or business that will be successful however you define success in your life. When you've mastered these lessons and have the necessary knowledge, power, and experience under your belt, it's time to help others become the best version of themselves.

We live in a broken world. People are broken. If you take the time to get to know anyone authentically, you will see the wounds. We all have something inside that digs away at our confidence and fosters doubt and fear. And healing is hard work. It takes deliberate focus and self-awareness. In understanding this, I realized that helping others heal is very important. I believe that every person is perfectly created by God and in his image. The greatest two commandments I have are to love the Lord with all my heart, mind, and soul and to love others as I love myself. Because you're created in God's image and I love the Lord, then there's something in you I love. It is a natural calling for me to love you.

Too often in business, leaders do not love those they lead until they generate results. This approach has become commonplace and, when it goes too far, tends to create toxic environments. Results are not attached to the love and care of your team members. A leader's responsibility is to help bring out the best in those they lead. It's not just for the benefit of the business, workplace, or environment. It's to use the strength they have created while becoming a leader to help others reach their best personal potential. If a business is going to grow, so must the people who make up that business. Good leaders invest the time and money to help team members advance in their personal and professional lives.

> Good leaders invest the time and money to help team members advance in their personal and professional lives.

In 1943, psychologist Abraham Maslow developed a hierarchy of needs that all human beings have. The most basic physiological needs of food, shelter, rest, safety, etc. make up the foundation of the hierarchy. Safety needs follow, like personal security, employment, resources, health, and property. These first two levels are table stakes in the employment you are offering. Great businesses are able to engage people in the next three levels. Love and belonging is next, where people experience friendship, family, and a sense of community.

Esteem follows, bringing respect, self-worth, status, recognition, strength, and freedom. The final part of the hierarchy is self-actualization, where people are reaching their full potential. Businesses and leaders who create environments where people can move through these levels consistently will transform people and communities.

There is often a disconnect in business today between leadership and those who make up their teams. Leaders and owners exist in the higher levels of Maslow's hierarchy, where they experience prestige and accomplishment and tend to focus only on these things. They don't realize that those they lead may not have many of their basic or psychological needs fulfilled. When you've reached a stage of the hierarchy, you have a responsibility to provide effective development for other people who are working to attain the same stage or above. The only way to accomplish both goals is to throw a rope back to others and bring them to where you are and beyond.

This can be risky, though. Sometimes you throw a rope to someone and it breaks, they let go of it, or they make a mistake. Fear of having this happen and looking bad to others can hold back a leader who is stuck in the mire of their personal esteem needs. Instead of taking risks on ideas or people who don't have as much experience or standing, they listen only to other leaders or hire people with big résumés or prestige. They think this approach is their best bet to deliver success to the business. In my experience, the most effective programs and ideas resulting in transformational growth have come from the people who are on the front lines every day, not from executives or leaders. So it makes sense to help people develop to lead your business.

Helping those who are working to reach their full potential is not only good business but also the right thing to do. It's not acceptable to me to win without others around me winning. I'm on a journey, and I'm trying to take a lot of people with me: clients, team members, vendors, and others. And I try my best to prioritize servanthood and stewardship over "leading." Transformational leadership begins by focusing on loving and serving those you lead. This means listening, asking questions, finding and celebrating the value others are creating, providing the support and development your teams need to grow, and learning from the stories all these actions create.

A Lesson from Darin

I will never forget Darin, a salesperson who ended up at my lunch table on his first day of work. I was the CEO of Defenders at the time and engaged in a conversation with four other people at the table. We were discussing the business, goals, and what was going on with the company in general. Darin didn't have to engage with me. He could've sat quietly and just listened. Instead, he asked me directly, "What is the one most important thing I need to do to be successful here?" I asked him if he had any sales experience and if he was any good at it. He answered yes to both questions. I took a moment to think before asking if he had a passport. When he curiously said no, I told him the most important thing to do to be successful at Defenders was to get a passport.

I explained to Darin that he would learn about the process for making sales and being deliberate about his work and growth. This would lead him to awards and opportunities to travel the world. A good way to start his new job would be to get a passport and keep it in sight every day. That simple thing would make it easier for Darin to stay focused on achieving his goals. What I didn't know was that Darin didn't have a home or a car at the time. He was sleeping on a friend's couch five miles from the office. He walked to work every day, five miles one way during February in Indiana. And he worked the graveyard shift. Darin's basic needs of food, shelter, and safety were not being met.

Four years later, I got an email from Darin one day at 5:00 a.m. He wanted to share what that first conversation had done for him. Darin got his passport, a passport to an amazing journey of becoming his best self. He began winning sales very quickly and was able to move into an apartment close to the office. Then he won a car in a sales contest. He sold the car and paid a full year's rent. Darin didn't need a car for security and safety; not having to worry about rent was more important to him. As Darin continued to work at Defenders, he blasted through every goal he had. In the course of five years, he had taken a Sales Superstar Award trip every year and used his passport every time. The morning he emailed me, he was sitting at the airport and was on his way to his third mission trip in the Dominican Republic to build a home for a family who didn't have one.

I still tear up whenever I think about Darin's story. He was at a low point in his life when we had that first conversation. By counseling him to get a passport as a tool for success, I was saying in my own way, "You've got what it takes. You can win here. Let's plan to win and prepare ourselves this way." That one encounter turned something on for him that empowered him to create beauty and abundance he could share with others. Because he knew a thing or two about homelessness and poverty, he focused on projects that helped people in impoverished countries.

Darin was sharing his abundance with others, and it did not surprise me. He was always so helpful to everyone around him. I remember that he would tell new salespeople, "Marcia told me the most important thing was to get a passport when you start here." He volunteered to participate in company service projects that brought teams to Mexico to build homes for families. Those trips gave him life-changing experiences he never had before, and the internal transformation spilled over into how he worked for his team and the business. The more motivated Darin was to win at his job, the more the company grew, and the more we could all share with others.

In business, there are people who just show up, do their jobs, watch the clock, and punch out. You don't get as much performance out of team members who don't find value in their work and are just trying to fulfill basic needs. However, if that same person is working for a well-run business with good processes and development of people, they can find purpose in what they do and take pride in how they do their jobs. The goal is to get the right people into the right seats and engage them with processes and systems that produce good outcomes. Then you have created an environment for joyful employment, where your team creates and shares abundance, is paid well, and enjoys experiences and benefits that make them want to do their best for their family, their leader, and the company.

Darin's story is a case study of the impact that this kind of transformative leadership can have. Working helped him fulfill basic needs, such as healthcare, food, water, warmth, and rest. He was consistently making more money than he ever had before, which enabled him to get an apartment and a more secure environment. Darin could have been satisfied with just this amount of success. But the continued support he got from leadership at Defenders motivated him to do more.

Psychologically, Darin felt like he had value and was accepted by those of us who worked at Defenders. He was able to experience feelings of prestige and accomplishment when he made good money, earned award trips, and was recognized for his contributions. This kind of support and development elevated Darin to experience self-actualization and engage in creative activities. All his needs were being met through his work. For the first time in his life, Darin had abundance he could share with others. He chose to throw a rope to people who had been where he was, whether it was a new hire, a colleague, or a homeless family. As a result, many, many lives have been changed through this one life.

Leading with Humility

There is a difference between being a boss and being a leader. Being a boss is about managing and entitlement. The mindset is "I'm your boss and these are the things I want you to do." Leadership is about creating abundance. This gets back into the love, serve, lead mission in the first part of this book. A leader's mindset is "I love you. I'm here for you. We're going to win together. How can I help you? I'm motivated to serve." When you can establish that love and serve clearly, people give you permission to lead them. Once you have permission to lead, you'll get so much more done than you would by trying to manage people.

You really can't serve others without having a certain amount of humility as a leader. God gave us dominion over creation, not one another. Transformational leaders concentrate on having dominion over work, not people. When you approach leadership with humility, it's easier to see the value in others and to guide their developmental path around the areas in which they're strong. You learn about the people you lead, see them as a whole person in a whole job, and value how they're created and what they're capable of doing. You want to learn from your team members and give them opportunities to teach you.

Some view humility in business as allowing yourself to be walked over. I view it as a continuum. On one side, you have the person who says, "I know everything and can do it all myself. I'm the boss and you all report to me. I am entitled to have your respect." This person has unhealthy self-esteem. On the far opposite side, you have the person who says, "I'm not worthy. I never do anything right. I don't want to try this again because I made mistakes last time and failed." This person has unhealthy low self-esteem. Neither one of these mindsets work for leadership.

In the middle of this continuum, you have the transformational leader. This person flawlessly balances self-esteem and is a humble servant leader. They believe they are perfectly created to deliver value and serve others while moving their business forward. They know they have what it takes to win today, and past experience will help them do the same in the future. Transformational leaders are always continuing to learn and develop themselves, not to move up in the business but to better serve others.

I have a reputation for being an avid reader. Back in the days when I had a three-hour commute to work, I would listen to audiobooks. At home and in my spare time, I would read anything and everything I could on all kinds of subjects. I would go through fifty or more books a year during this time in my life, almost a book every week. This passion I had for reading wasn't about becoming smarter or getting a promotion. My goal with each book was to find or generate ideas that could help others. When I read something in the construct of serving others, ideas and solutions came more quickly and freely to me.

Transformational leaders are missional but not mercenary in how they lead. Being missional means you are called to the space you're in to serve people and get a certain result in a set point in time. You accomplish this mission by letting your best self come out through the fulfillment of that work. Humility is the thread through all this that enables you to be missional in your leadership style.

Those who are mercenary approach leadership in a way that is primarily concerned with making money at the expense of others. They are always seeking what's next or bigger or better. This kind of inward focus creates stress within yourself and a conflict between perfection and progress. In that environment, there is no humility, and no one wins as a direct result.

Leaders with humility address the spiritual, emotional, and physical well-being of their team. They acknowledge strengths, notice challenges, and then put support mechanisms in place to meet their needs. Your role as a business leader is not one of entitlement and power to squeeze the value out of your people into your business. It's to humbly empower and inspire the value out of your people and into the world to bless others.

Value and Support Your Team

There is a silent, unwritten covenant between a leader and a team member. The leader agrees to provide the support to the team member, who also agrees to provide a service. How you live up to your responsibilities in this covenant defines what kind of leader you are. When you give your team resources, feedback, attention, and time in a way that comes from your heart, you show them that they are valued and important. The result is a happier team that does better work, has greater confidence and creativity, has higher retention rates, and generates larger financial returns.

I learned a long time ago that improving customer experience begins with paying attention to what is going on with the people on your team. If I'm not treating my people right, giving them the support they need, and truly valuing their work, I am not serving them well. And you can never get to a good customer experience without having a good internal team experience. If you're rude to your children, they're going to be rude to others. The same applies here. But if you invest time, effort, and heart into creating a supportive environment that makes people feel valued, teams amplify that positive experience into their interactions with customers.

A transformational leader serves the needs of and engages with their teams. They know their names and stories and treat them as whole people who have lives inside and outside of work. They're observant and conscious of how the team's work is performed so that they can provide positive feedback and spot challenges. If they notice when a team member takes one action and good things happen in response, they share that observation. When a team member is assigned a particular account and their work leads to a specific growth result, they celebrate that win. Being able to see in concrete terms how their work is making a difference is an incredible motivator. It boosts feelings of confidence and belonging, which makes them want to do more of the things that generated those emotions.

When Dave and I first started working together and he was my client, he would visit the office once a month. He met some of our people on his first visit and remembered those people's names and some of their details the second time he came in. He did this every time he came to the office. I would watch him walking around my business, exchanging comments, calling people by name, asking how a daughter was doing in school or a son on the baseball team. My people latched onto that. I was their leader and here's this client coming in and creating an immediate expression of affection between them. The action of remembering names and details created such a powerful result that I adopted it as part of my own leadership priorities.

Another simple yet powerful part of valuing people is showing them that you are thankful and appreciative of them. The more specific and timely you can be with your thanks, the better. People need to hear you say something good to them eight times before they can accept one piece of coaching. Making these deposits all the time is important because at some point you will need to correct a behavior or an outcome. When that time comes, you serve the team member by not letting their weaknesses become such a focus that they overshadow their strengths. Come from a place of appreciation as you coach to correct. But really focus on where the person is strong because that's where they're going to add the most value to your business. You're not going to get anywhere picking apart people's gaps.

For example, when I was CEO at Defenders and the company grew by $100 million in eighteen months, it wasn't because I was leaning on the teams, cutting pay, or giving them extra work. It was because I knew their names and their stories, was appreciative and thankful, listened to their ideas on how we could do better, and then organized them around those ideas. By engaging people in the things they told me needed to be done, everybody went in the same direction and got 1 or 2 percent better results. That may not seem like a lot, but when you have twenty-six hundred people around the flywheel generating 2 percent more than before, you get $100 million in growth in eighteen months.

At Valve+Meter, we have several company-wide meetings throughout the year. I see these as opportunities to show our teams that they are seen, they are heard, and they are valued. I know that as an employer, I made a decision at some point to choose a team member for a particular job. But they make a choice every day to share their time and talent with me. For every meeting, I ask team members to tell me why they continue to say yes to working for Valve+Meter. Some of the more recent responses include the following:

- "When I had health challenges, you all stuck to the core values like I have never seen."
- "This is a job you can make your own."
- "The CEO knows my name."
- "Our three hundred percent increase in organic traffic for this client saved jobs. That's something to be proud of."
- "I wanted to be in a company where I could influence outcomes. This is it."
- "It's rare to have the voice in your company we have here at Valve+Meter."
- "I love the clients who hire us for growth so they can pass an asset to the next generation. Watching it happen fills my heart."

Comments like these tell me we are doing something right in how we serve the teams we lead. I encourage open and honest communication from team members and work to show them that their voices are taken seriously. I notice when they're winning, where they're making breakthroughs, and where things aren't going right. It's not unusual for me to check on what's happening with them personally. I want to see how they're winning in parenting, marriage, community service, and the circles they move in. It gives me a lot of joy when one of my team members buys a new house, has a baby, or takes a trip they've been planning for a long time but hadn't been able to manage. I like to hear about the abundance they've created and are able to share with others.

Enable Your Team to Grow

The best and most effective teams value personal and professional development. That's because as a business grows, so must the people who make it work. A business that invests in continued development opportunities is cultivating teams able to drive the business forward and win in ways you may never had imagined. People are hungry for good leadership. When they find it inside your walls, it's incredibly powerful.

Dave knew how valuable development was for the future of Defenders. His mindset was the company needed to be continually growing, and the best way to do that was to enable the rest of us to continually grow as well. Dave and I would go to leadership conferences or workshops together. We would read books at the same time and discuss them. As I think through my career with him, Dave invested around $250,000 in my development. He never looked at it like he was taking a risk in spending $10,000 to send me to take a course. He knew by my track record that he could send me to that course, and I'd bring him back a million-dollar idea that worked. And I did.

I find too many leaders are overly focused on talent attraction and retention, then overlook how much value they get in providing opportunities for development. There is fear that money spent on professional development will be wasted if the team member learns what they need, then takes their skills to another company. So they overrotate toward talent retention instead of talent development. And while I'm not saying it isn't important, I also don't think losing talent after investing in their growth is something to fear. It's not my goal in business to hire people and then hang on to them at a rate of pay or in a job role that might be less than what they're valued at somewhere else. Those who work for me are not my property. I don't own them. I'm just in stewardship of them while they're here.

If I say that my business has the authority and the right to fire somebody because I'm not getting results or I no longer need that position, I have to agree that the team member has the same ability. If they're not getting what they need from me or we no longer fit their career path, then they have the right to fire me. But if we can meet in this space where we agree that I'm on their side and they're here to add value, we can get to a place where we trust each other. I agree to provide the support and resources they need to grow as well as acceptable pay and benefits. They agree to bring their talents, knowledge, and skills. And together, we grow.

Because Valve+Meter is a successful marketing agency that's getting great results and has a reputation for investing in developing our people, they are highly sought after by other companies. Team members will get offers, some of which I can't compete with financially. The value is not in my business. It's in the person I have invested time, money, and experience building up to be ready for the next step in their journey, whenever that might be. I don't feel that this is a bad thing.

I've had a couple of situations when I've had people tell me up front that they're going to leave. How would you react if someone on your team said this to you? If you're a transformational leader, you'll want to find out what the need really is and help them satisfy it. I actually like it when team members come to me with this news. Then I can help them find another place that will enable them to grow beyond my limitations.

Last year, I took a team member, Zach, to an event I was speaking at and introduced him to the audience. I told them Zach was doing great work for us at Valve+Meter, but we just weren't growing fast enough for him to get to the position he wants to be in for a career. I gave him a public recommendation to anyone in the audience who might have an opportunity for him on their team.

He didn't get a job offer that day, but he made several connections and stayed with Valve+Meter. For the next six months, he spent a lot of time studying and learning a new set of skills, which we encouraged. Before he knew it, we had a position ready that we really needed him to fill and that was just the right fit for his goals. But even if the outcome had led Zach to another company, the support and encouragement we provided him to get where he wanted to be was all worth the effort.

This is kind of a radical way of thinking, and you may not agree with me on this. Spending the time and energy to help others grow is the bedrock of transformational leadership. If you go to your grave having been successful and you didn't take anybody with you, there were opportunities missed. The dash, the space between the birth and death dates on our tombstones, shouldn't be about us being successful. It should be about ful-

> *Spending the time and energy to help others grow is the bedrock of transformational leadership.*

filling what we were sent here to do and how much we accomplished. In business, that means being a servant leader who provides for their teams and helps build a culture where everyone wins. Doing this with others and winning together is a life well lived.

TOOLS FOR GROWTH

VIDEO: JOIN OUR TEAM
Scan the QR code or visit mathbeforemarketing.com/join

TOOLS FOR GROWTH

HARVESTING IDEAS

MY IDEAS FROM THIS CHAPTER

TOOLS FOR GROWTH

BEST PRACTICE:
HOW TO READ A BOOK

Scan the QR code or visit mathbeforemarketing.com/howtoreadabook

CHAPTER 9

HOW CULTURE TRANSFORMS BUSINESS

Culture eats strategy for breakfast.

—PETER DRUCKER

A friend of mine is the president of a company specializing in growing other businesses. A couple of years ago, she told me they will pass on taking on a client whose company has not grown for two or three years. This seemed counterintuitive to me. There should be lots of opportunities to help a business like that win more sales and grow. She explained that a business that has been stagnant for that long has institutionalized failure. So much time has passed since they've experienced growth that they've forgotten how to do it, how it feels, and what the benefits are. Those circumstances make it so much harder for her programs to work.

That's a powerful statement: if you haven't grown for two to three years, you have institutionalized failure. In the last chapter, I talked about how good leadership focused on growing people as well as the business is what leads to transformational results for everyone. This is the only way I know how to approach starting or working with a business because that was the kind of environment I learned in. I saw firsthand the impact that a people/growth-focused culture has on those who work there and on the bottom line. I also saw what happened when you take that kind of culture away.

In my career, I've experienced many broken cultures. And when you've been working for four decades, you've seen a lot. I've seen cultures

- of favoritism, where friends and family were elevated, the results were created by the frontline team members, and no one was promoted from within;
- where sexual impropriety was the norm and the company imploded with the advent of sexual harassment laws;
- of drinking, where the owner was an alcoholic who held court at the bar with the men on the team every evening. It wasn't until his twenty-second DUI that he was put in jail. Thank you, MADD, for finally rising to influence over drunk driving laws; and
- deeply imbedded in male leadership. Even though I had far exceeded all expectations, an unqualified man was given my job and I was demoted to a frontline position. He knew so little about what he was doing that I was expected to advise him or do his work for him.

I'd like to think that these are extreme abuses of power and not ones still in use today. At least, this is my hope. The truth is that there are still toxic environments or behaviors that may be subtle, but they are still destructive. I've said before that we live in a broken world with broken people, and the workplace is just a small part of it. Leaders become tone deaf to the damage they're creating for people when they take from others in order to give to themselves. The long-term impact of this is that a business will limit its potential growth and profitability as foundations of trust crumble.

To me, it's just sad and sick that somewhere there's a trade-off for people where it's acceptable to treat folks poorly because you employ them. There are plenty of people out there who've created massive wealth and treat people correctly. The two outcomes are not mutually exclusive.

I believe that my role as a business owner is to enable and encourage people for however long they are with me and to prepare them for their next step in life. When you're sitting inside some big corporate cog and no one is giving you purpose or sharing with you meaningful results from your work, you're in a soul suck. But when you can go home at the end of the day and tell your loved ones that your work saved 20 percent of the jobs at a company or solved a problem for a family, you can't wait to go back and do it again and again.

So far in our transformational journey, I've shown you how taking a servant mindset can help you grow as an individual. You've learned that, as a transformational leader, you can take the abundance you create and use it to build up others. Now you'll see how you can transform your whole business by building an engaging culture of supportive growth for your team and others you work with.

What Is Culture?

Ask most people what their company culture is and they'll point to the annual Christmas party or awards event. There may be a family day or service project they can participate in. What they don't understand is that these are just events that take place as part of their business culture. They don't

Culture is a commonality that represents what you value as a company.

define it. Culture is a commonality that represents what you value as a company. It's found in the everyday workings of the business, the feeling and nature of the relationships within and outside of it, and the collective personality of the company.

Culture is felt by every team member, customer, vendor, and influencer. It's the space you give the internal and external teams you support. It's in how you hire and fire, promote, recognize, and affirm. It's how you choose to grow yourself and your leaders. The clients you take on, the promises you make to them, and your accountability and transparency are all part of your culture. It's also in the kinds of relationships you form with vendors, the value you give them as part of your business success, and how you treat them in both good and challenging times.

In short, culture is all of it together—that people part of your business. Culture is not some nebulous cloud created by an executive team and dropped on people. It is a living, growing element of a business. It's the sum of all of us working together with shared values defining how we show up personally, to others, clients, vendors, influencers, the communities we serve in, and the world. Culture is you. Culture is me. Culture is us.

Culture typically is founded on the deep core values of the CEO's or owner's vision when they started the business and what they wanted it to do in the world. Many owners are running a business for the first time and have neither developed nor even thought about culture before. They typically jump right in with the "doing of things" and then later start to ask, "Who are we now, and where are we?" That is important work, and there are lots of great systems and methodologies out there to help with that. But all of that really needs to develop as a result of defining who you are as a business and what your intention in the world is, which is the culture piece.

If you don't define the values and set the tone for your business's culture, one will naturally form in reaction to leadership and expectations. Toxic cultures often form under these circumstances, resulting in losses in human capital, productivity, revenue, and possibly reputation. You can avoid this by placing culture first in your priorities. Use clearly defined core values and a strong internal culture as the bedrock of everything you do as a business. If you haven't already done this, I encourage you to get there as quickly as possible.

When you're not prioritizing a strong, healthy culture that touches everyone associated with the business, you're losing money. Whether it's through reduced productivity, lost clients from poor experiences with teams, being fired by vendors that aren't treated decently, inefficiencies that aren't discovered because attention isn't being paid correctly, or any other of a thousand ways a toxic or unsupportive culture hurts business, your profitability and growth are being held back. And you're well on your way to institutionalizing failure.

Culture is the heart of your company and is all about the people. I think this is the piece that gets missed too often. People are what make your business successful or cause it to struggle. You can say you have great culture, but do your people think so? If you don't interact with people and you don't care about the whole of what's going on with them, you end up with just part of a person performing in your business, not the whole person.

When you have the whole person in your business, what you get is a highly engaged team member who's going to be a healthier worker for you over a longer period of time. This is why investing in a supportive, people-centric culture valuing the talents and development of individuals is one of the most powerful ways to attain transformative growth for your business.

Valve+Meter's Culture Story

I was very intentional in building the kind of culture I wanted to have at Valve+Meter. Right before I was set to launch the business, I took a week off to go to San Diego and have the perfect single woman's vacation. I planned to go sailing, play golf at Torrey Pines, visit the zoo and SeaWorld, and have some wonderful dinners. By the time I got to my hotel, I thought I was coming down with a cold. The next thing I knew, I had a full-blown case of the flu that knocked me flat for the whole vacation.

When I look back on how that trip unfolded, I feel like God created the space for me to be still and listen to what was about to happen with Valve+Meter. Stuck in bed without much to do, I wrote pages of statements about what I wanted the culture to be and what I thought the core values were. Working through what your business's core values are is always a really good place to start. If you try to develop too much about the product, the business, the pricing, and the customers before you get to core values, then you're going to identify values that fit those things instead of what you really want to create and are called to do.

As part of my process for creating Valve+Meter's core values, I wrote pages about how we would treat people, finance, compensation, clients, team members, culture, events, networks, tithing, profits, and abundance. These were all the things I wanted this business to do. Coming out of that, I was pretty locked into the idea that when we love people well, we get a desire to serve them. When we love and serve people well, they give us permission to lead them. And when we have permission to lead, we get transformational growth. Love, serve, and transform seemed to be what the culture of Valve+Meter was going to be about, and we opened the business with those core values at the center of everything.

During the first few weeks that Valve+Meter was in business, we had conversations about what we were about to do as a company and the marketing problem we wanted to solve. It always came back to the same point: businesses aren't being treated fairly when it comes to marketing. The way they buy marketing is broken, and the way agencies sell marketing is broken. A lot of companies get stuck in long-term agreements where the agency is agnostic to the results they're delivering. They're just trying to sell something to the business and keep that agreement for as long as they can. There were all kinds of things like this that I thought needed to be addressed in order to create fairness, and so "be just" quickly became an additional core value for us.

After a couple of years, we started to realize that a lot of what we do at Valve+Meter deals with data and analytics, creating campaigns that work, being smart about what we do, making good strategy, testing, and adjusting things as we go along. So we added "think" to our core values. It's important to note here that though I am the owner and CEO of the business, I strive to be a servant leader. Ensuring that I get the foundation for my agency right was important to me. The only way that I knew I would get there was going through this process and bringing in my team members to include their voices in the conversations. The result of this collaborative relationship is the five core values we have today:

1. **Think:** We focus and find a way forward. We view everything as a hypothesis and rely on data to inform decisions, tests, and processes. We think about how we can accomplish things rather than focusing on why we cannot. We believe that opportunities are always greater than obstacles. And we only succeed as a team.

2. **Love:** We act in the long-term best interests of another. We love what we do. We strive to be our best for ourselves, our teams,

and our clients. We are grateful for the work our coworkers do to push our team and clients forward. We both require and provide autonomy and trust. We empathize and love people where they are, not where they could be.

3.   **Serve:** We meet expectations and then go the extra mile. Our clients' successes are our successes. We say yes to big goals, big challenges, and the opportunity to go our own way. We approach conversations with humility and the knowledge that it is a privilege to serve. We give abundantly because abundance moves mountains. We have a bias toward action. And we answer the damn phone.

4.   **Transform:** We create dramatic change. We strive to be irreplaceable. We exist to drive transformational growth. It's not for the faint of heart. We believe that change is inevitable while growth is intentional. We know that traction transforms. We are fearless and deliberately do things that make us uncomfortable. And we know that growth is always calling.

5.   **Be just:** We are fair and accountable. We do no harm. We listen, then seek first to understand and be understood second. We respect differences and value all perspectives. We believe that accountability creates traction and that there are times when we are wrong. But failure is an option because we learn from our mistakes.

Each of these values details the shared beliefs we have at Valve+Meter as a company and as a team—our culture. The values guide our attitudes toward work and the choices we make in accomplishing our tasks. They also apply to how we view and treat each other within the company, our clients, our vendors, and the organizations we interact with in our community. By reading this list, you can get a clear sense of what it's like to work for and with Valve+Meter. You'll also be able to determine whether who we are and how we do things is the right fit for you. Whether you're a prospective client, vendor, employee, or partner, we want you to know what our company is all about before choosing to work with us.

How Culture Influences Business

Once you establish a clear path for core values and culture, you're ready to start talking about what they look like when applied to the people involved with the business, such as teams, clients, operations, etc. You'll want to build your systems to align with those core values and processes that ensure they're being applied. This line of thought will lead you to establishing a purpose and mission for the business. Getting this right is very important because it acts like a guiding star for your teams and clients. They know that working with you is going to accomplish something specific in their world. Something that's valuable to them and motivates them to do their best for you in return.

It's easier for culture to be good in businesses that are growing. When businesses are growing, opportunities start opening up for people to be promoted and learn new skills. Profits rise, benefits improve, and what we can do as a business with and for our people also increases. If you're not growing, you can't do those things. When you're flatlining or going backward, you're either intentionally cutting people because you're declining or you're trying to hold the position you have in the market. There's also a high likelihood that the people on your team will leave on their own to be able to get their next opportunity. To the people you need to make your business successful, you have little to offer.

I recently spoke with someone who worked for me for more than a decade. He just started a new job and told me that everyone around him is managing and not leading. He can see them focusing on the process and numbers, the grind and march, discipline, feedback, write-ups, and all that. They're not using the vision to give team members something to march toward. They don't understand that by connecting the heart with the mind and modeling the way to do so, it makes everyone's experience easier and more joyful. Healthier communication focused on how we all win together in a meaningful culture drives consistent energy, results, and innovation.

I was humbled by this conversation. This person's experience taught him how a supportive, people-focused culture interwoven into every process and system within a business can make you want to achieve more. He has experienced growth, abundance, and wealth as a result of being a part of that kind of environment. Stepping into a new job where there is little to no culture providing support to those workers exposes a weaker, disjointed business. I expect that his new company will end up losing someone of great value because they don't know how to do culture right.

When a healthy culture is implemented in a business, it will help guide all your decisions. You'll be better able to go after your ideal clients and be crystal clear on what you're selling to them. I often have businesses who want to buy a list of marketing tactics from me. They are not interested in measurable results. We pass on these opportunities. The reason is simple: the client wasn't a good fit for what Valve+Meter is all about.

Another example is in how we work with our clients. We look to our core values to guide us in identifying opportunities and addressing challenges as we build client relationships. If the client won't share data with us (once in a while we run into that), we can't create transparency. For Valve+Meter, it would feel like we are not able to do our work correctly, and it typically causes a client to doubt they are getting results. We want to be just in our dealings. Being just means that we want to handle the marketing investment in a productive way: get the data, find the solution, and act on it. We wouldn't let that tension continue because it goes against our values. Instead, we work with the client to get the transparency we need so that everyone can win. That really is our goal as a company: enabling everyone we touch to create abundance that transforms. And it's our culture that fuels our ability to do it.

Leading in a Strong Culture

I talked a lot in the last chapter about how leadership should begin from a desire to serve. Servant leadership must remain at the core of how you and your business leaders implement culture. If you can build effective culture and prioritize people development, you're going to hit financial and growth metrics that deliver success. It's just much harder for you to do if all you're addressing are the things that have obvious financial impact. When it becomes about hitting a number, regardless of what is going on with the people involved with that number, the outcome shifts, and success is so much harder to get.

Leaders in a strong culture know you manage processes and lead people. There's a difference in that. A business process is something you use to get a predictable result. You want your people to follow that business process, so you lead them in doing so. If you're making them feel like bad human beings because something isn't going right somewhere in the process or the results have changed, you're not being a servant leader.

There are no "bad" people. There are bad processes. The core values in a strong culture provide you with a way to lead your people to success by managing the processes that relate to them. To do this, you must do the following.

Analyze all the processes impacting the result by asking these questions in this order:

- Is the current process being followed?
- Is there a break in the process?
- Do we need a new process?
- Determine what needs adjustment to get the outcomes you're looking for.
- Test the new or modified process to ensure that it delivers the right outcomes.
- Then teach the new process to your team.

There are good and bad elements in every culture. Our job as leaders is to lift up the things that are good about the culture and push down those that are bad. I'm not saying that you should ignore the bad things. Quite the opposite, actually. Not speaking up about problems or not being completely honest about what's going on is a surefire way to a toxic work environment. As a leader, you want to mitigate the risks by looking at what could be done to make what's negative not be an issue or, at the very least, reduce the impact it has. We also want to make sure the things that are working in the culture get talked about a lot and that we're continually elevating those things in a logical, not manipulative, way.

It's impossible to get everything right 100 percent of the time, especially as a leader. That's because culture is all about complex people with unique personalities. Their personal values and the ways that they interact with the world may not match up to yours. What you're trying to drive home with your company culture doesn't always show up or feel the same for every person. It's a constant learning and development process. Even at my stage of development and experience, I still make mistakes.

When I was ready to create Valve+Meter, it had been decades since I had built a start-up company. I had forgotten things about what's involved with running a new business. There were many challenges, such as taking a new concept to market as well as new marketing and financial models. It was my first time doing a lot of this type of work.

I had not owned this type of an agency before. Even though I knew what good leadership should have been, there was a lot more bad leadership coming from me during that time. I cast my goals way beyond what we were able to hit, which frustrated people and caused those who believed in the business to think we just couldn't get it right. Those first couple of years were the worst representation of how I think culture should run.

Coming back to serving rather than leading helped us change course. I began following all the steps and strategies I've talked about in this book. I relearned how to be a small business owner by being grateful, building my own skills and knowledge, and investing appropriately in people, benefits, development, and training. I poured all of that into how I led and continue to do so every day that I come to work. I interact and have relationships with the people who work on my team, and I keep my responsibility for serving them and helping them grow at the forefront of everything I do.

I love our quarterly all-team meetings because I get to check in with them on how our culture is doing. I ask everyone to write down why they joined Valve+Meter and why they continue to choose us every day. It's a good reminder to all of us to think about why we threw in with this motley crew. Two or three people will then share their stories with the whole team. In a different environment, they might want to keep their time addressing us to a minimum. But here, they unpack whole stories that are just precious and sweet.

For instance, one of my team members recently said this about his reason for working at Valve+Meter: "Changing jobs is terrifying. Working with the wrong people is dangerous." He had read that quote in a book a few weeks before I called him about joining the team. I had worked with him at another place, and he already knew a lot of people who work here. I knew he was the right fit for the position I had open, but it was up to him to choose to share his talent with us. He told me that when he started to think about who he was currently working with and who he could be working with at Valve+Meter, it was an easy choice to make.

I think that says a lot about the impact that a supportive and strong culture has on a business. Valuing people, knowing their names, saying thank you, and being aware of what's going on with your teams helps you be a good leader in that culture. You don't have to necessarily go super deep. But you do have to honor the souls who are walking through your doors every day trying to contribute to the value of your organization. And I feel like we're on a good track the way that we've been intentional about building the kind of culture we have.

It's only thanks to a lot of hard work as a team that we have built a unique marketing agency and get transformational results for clients. Our people are growing and transforming as well. Folks are succeeding, getting promoted, buying homes and cars, having babies, and saving for retirement. Our team members are thriving because of the culture we've intentionally built. By the time this book is published, we will be pacing to be a $10 million agency in just six years. Our customer retention is really high. Our results for our clients are transformational. And because serving is so ingrained into our being as a business, we are sharing from that abundance to transform the world.

TOOLS FOR GROWTH

VIDEO: CLIENT STORIES

Scan the QR code or visit mathbeforemarketing.com/stories

TOOLS FOR GROWTH

HARVESTING IDEAS

MY IDEAS FROM THIS CHAPTER

CHAPTER 10

THE JOY OF GIVING

Test me in this and see if I will not throw open the
floodgates of heaven and pour out so much blessing
that there will not be room enough to store it.

—MALACHI 3:10 (NIV)

A ll meaningful change starts on the inside and works its way out. We've been talking about how to develop your skills as an individual and as a transformational leader so that you can better serve others. We've looked at how important good stewardship of internal culture is to a business's health and ability to grow. Now we need to think about what else you are in stewardship of and where you can help others share that same blessing. One good place to do that is in your business with your team members.

A few days before starting Valve+Meter, I spent a whole week writing page upon page of what I wanted the culture to be, and I dedicated a whole page to what giving and serving should look like. It included service projects that we would do as a company. Our people would lead those projects, volunteer with causes that spoke to them, and serve on the boards of whatever organizations they were drawn to. I wanted to tithe 10 percent from our profits and engage our team in the activity of sharing abundance from work with others. All those things were something important to me that I wanted to implant into the basic heartbeat of our organization.

I will often read that your business should give back because social impact matters for retention and attraction of employees. That feels self-serving to me. If you're just doing it to check a box so you can be a good employer or get the best employees and keep them for a long time, then you're missing out. You're just getting a fraction of what's available to you, not only regarding finances and business growth but also in your happiness, joy, and impact as a business leader. The moment you make giving about better business results, you cut out a lot of the value.

As business leaders, we have an obligation to help others grow as holistic human beings. If someone is in my care inside my business and I'm not doing this, I will have not done for them what others did for me while I was on my own growth journey. It would also mean I'm not exposing them to a lot of the things that have given me great joy in my life, and that seems selfish to me. I want to enable my team to have opportunities to lead service projects, learn different ways to give and help, be part of making decisions about who to help, and understand the concept of how tithing becomes a blessing for them.

I infuse giving within my business because those who make up my team are whole people working in a whole job. By giving and sharing with people the blessings, tithes, and support we have all worked together as a team to create, I'm developing whole people in a whole job. Neglecting giving strategies in developing people is unacceptable to me. I want our team to participate in giving, because we are on this journey together. When team members go out and grow through service

> As business leaders, we have an obligation to help others grow as holistic human beings.

and giving, they share their experiences with us, and I grow too. I've learned new insights and new ways that they're encountering these ministries. This is meaningful to me.

In this final lesson, I'm going to show you how you can infuse your business with a spirit of giving. In my experience, I think a lot of the results and growth we've experienced at Valve+Meter are because we have been very committed to giving our time, talent, and treasure from the very beginning. I want to show you how you can do the same thing by developing a model for how your business will give in an effective and scalable way. Then I'll show you how you can amplify those efforts with your influence. And along the way, I will share with you some of the amazing stories of abundance, transformation, and blessings from God I have seen by making giving a priority in my life.

Create a Model for Giving

There are a lot of ways to infuse giving and serving into a business. The key is to dial into the heart and soul of your organization and to think about what kind of structure and priorities make the most sense. Think of giving in terms of time, talent, and treasure.

- **Time:** Your time has value, and often it is the most meaningful gift of giving. It may also be the hardest thing for you to part with. Rocking a sick baby in the hospital, packing groceries at the food pantry, tutoring a child, being a Big Brother or Big Sister to a teenager, visiting prisons, nursing homes, or shelters, or whatever it is you are called to do is a manifestation of love.
- **Talent:** Each of us has special talents we can use to serve others. A gift for financial wisdom can be given by helping a domestic abuse shelter create a five-year financial plan. A gift for teaching could be given to help adults learn to read or get a

GED. A gift for marketing can be given to create a marketing strategy to attract foster parents. The gift for baking could be given to a homeless shelter. A gift for plumbing can be put to good use at Habitat for Humanity. The gift of leadership is needed greatly on nonprofit boards.

- **Treasure:** Let's be clear. God doesn't need your money. It all belongs to him. He wants your heart. He is inviting you into a life of joy through generosity. Giving makes you a participant in what God is doing in people's lives for kingdom impact. With tithing, giving 10 percent of your income is the standard. Giving more than 10 percent is an offering. And in my experience, you can't out-give God.

Start with an internal commitment goal of dedicating a certain number of hours, dollars, or people to some type of service. Then stick to that commitment. Set aside the time and resources needed to make it happen, work it into your annual budgets, and lead your people by setting the example. If they see that you are genuinely invested in giving, it will inspire them to lend their own hearts to the effort.

Service projects are a good place to start, and service is the gateway drug to giving. Figure out what service projects engage your team and enable you all to learn, grow, and develop together. At Valve+Meter, we have team members who help organize service projects, select what we should be doing, and decide where we should be serving. That's always good to see because they're learning to be givers while having life-altering experiences.

I had a team of eight people who chose to serve for a day at an orphanage that had a lot of older kids who were having trouble getting adopted. The organization that runs the orphanage is doing fantastic, difficult work from a heart that's trying to help the world heal. The team members who went to the orphanage were a bunch of young guys whose task was to play basketball with the boys. They were only supposed to be there for four hours, but they stayed for eight and came back with blisters on their feet, shoes worn through the soles, torn pants, and other signs of the joyful ruckus they'd experienced that day.

As I listened to the guys unpack their experiences, Ryan, one of the team members spoke up. He was one of those cool dudes who's always really professional, fashionable, and quietly reserved. He was not a very emotional person, yet there were tears streaming from Ryan's eyes as he told us about his day. He said he had never been so tired at the end of a day. But he was grateful for the blisters on his feet that would be there for days because he felt the impact of what his hours hanging out with these kids did for them.

One of the teachers at the orphanage told Ryan that these kids don't get male volunteers very often. Most people who come to help are women. The kids were so energized to hang out with young men, they wanted to be with them all day long. The profound need these children had for something Ryan had taken for granted his whole life hit him full force. He learned that he is a role model, a big brother, a kind person, a friend, and someone who can influence a life for the better. All it took was a few hours playing ball with a bunch of kids without fathers, family, or anyone else in the world. Having been confronted by this brokenness and learning that he could help make it better, he said, "Today, I learned what it means to be a man."

Thinking beyond service projects, there are a number of ways to make giving systemic in your business. Some include the following:

- Put into place plans and systems that set aside a percentage of profits to be donated.
- Create a program to match dollars that team members raise for things they care about.
- Give team members time off to volunteer.

- Help train team members in how to create donor-advised funds to manage giving.
- Recognize acts of service and giving and tell those stories.

Getting started may seem daunting, and bringing in strategic giving as a core focus to your business will mean change. It may be worth investing in some kind of training program for your team to learn about managing giving. There's a group called Generous Giving whose calling is to train people about generosity and giving. They host conversations about God and money in an environment that never asks you for anything in return. An organization like Generous Giving can help you develop your strategies so that they are sustainable and scalable. Check them out at GenerousGiving.org.

CHOOSE YOUR FOCUS

You can get lost in the mire of choosing where and how to focus your giving resources just from the sheer enormity of the need in the world. Start with identifying ways to serve and give that align with your company's core values, which are the heartbeat of your organization. Giving and service are the blood that's being pushed through that heartbeat. So thinking about how that aligns in the whole body of the business is something to put some serious thought into.

Regarding the work we do at Valve+Meter, I don't take every deal that comes into the agency. I have a strategic area from which I select accounts, and some things just don't fit us. The same applies to giving. There is a certain strategy we're going after. We don't need to do everything, so we use criteria based on our values and the type of giving we want to do as a team to consider whether to accept an opportunity. I try to focus on things that break cycles of poverty, addiction, and abuse because this is where my heart is. It's where I came from. As a company, we aim to enable transformative growth. We bring all of this together and focus our tithing on organizations and projects that can help make real change in someone's life. If that means helping out a local homeless shelter or school, building homes, tutoring, or some other project that fits the intention we've defined for giving, we'll consider it.

I've been involved with Youth with a Mission Homes of Hope in the San Diego Baja area of Mexico for more than a decade. Homes of Hope builds homes for the less fortunate with the help of teams from businesses, youth groups, churches, and other organizations. In two days' time, they can build a house for someone who doesn't have one. When you get there, you typically see somebody living out of a makeshift structure they've built out of cardboard, tarpaulins, plastic bags, and whatever wood they can scrape together. I've seen families who have dug a hole in the ground in and are covering themselves up at night with a tarpaulin. Within the two days you spend building a home there, you see a family transformed by generosity.

One family I helped build a home for was living out of a camper cap that's supposed to be attached to the back of a pickup truck. The camper part was sitting on their lot and this couple and their two teenage sons were living in it. I don't know how they were doing it, but their situation was better than many others. In this area, homes are just not there for a lot of people. Homes of Hope works in that space where they help people figure out how to acquire some land. Then they recruit business and youth groups, churches, and other organizations to come and build that home in partnership with the family. At the end of the two days, a family will have a sixteen-by twenty-foot home that's furnished and ready to move into.

The impact this group has is multifold. The sense of pride and ownership helps elevate the confidence of the family getting that home.

And having a house to grow up in completely changes the outcome of a child's life. Kids get sick a lot when they live on a dirt floor. Getting them onto a concrete floor helps improve their health, which enables them to go to school more consistently and get a better education. Then they can use that education to lift themselves and their families out of poverty. The impact is just so immediate, relevant, and transformative.

In 2022, I will make my twentieth trip to Mexico for one of these builds and have led hundreds of people down there over the years. It's always remarkable to see the difference in the volunteers between the time we're riding the bus from San Diego to Tijuana or Ensenada, and after the build when we're on our way back to the airport to return home. Going into the experience, the whole bus is thinking, "I'm going to give somebody a blessing; I'm doing a great thing." You can almost hear this little song going on in their heads. It's this vibration that says, "I'm about to do something that's relevant and important, and this is a great thing I'm doing."

On the return trips with the exact same people on that exact same bus, the vibe is completely different. People start to understand that they got more out of the experience than what they gave. Families become closer and everyone learns something about themselves and the way they lead or the way they relate to their families at home. The love they witnessed in the families they built a home for in Mexico taught them that. The family unit there is not unlike it is here; it's the economy that's unstable. It helps them understand the economic and environmental brokenness of the people they built the home for and change the preconceived ideas they had about these folks. Opening your mind to new ideas and possibilities the way you do on a trip like this is an immeasurable gift that profoundly affects your personal and professional lives. It's just another reason this work is so important for businesses to fold into their organizations.

INVOLVE THE TEAM

Bringing your team to the table to learn about and have a voice in how giving will be executed in your business is a really powerful thing. If you make all the decisions as a leadership team or as a business owner, you're cutting off a lot of the energy and engagement that can flow through your business from giving. Giving and serving are not going to appeal to everybody. But you need to be open to hearing from people in your business about it. As I said earlier in the book, the best ideas come from the front line. Make sure to include ways to involve your team in the structuring and conversations around building your model for giving.

Valve+Meter is an Entrepreneurial Operating System company where every team member has an opportunity to speak their voice into the business every single week. A lot of ideas are circulated as a result. We've developed the muscle to listen to these opportunities and hold to our giving strategy as we consider them. For example, we had a certain amount of profit I had set aside for tithing in 2021. My view is that the team earned the money and made the profits, so they needed to have stewardship over that and experience giving in its highest form. I gave the team eight highly vetted organizations fitting our agreed-upon giving strategy and asked them to vote on how they wanted the tithes to be distributed. They had time to research the groups and see which ones they connected with most.

After the voting was completed, we allocated the tithes according to the results. The donation went to each of the groups according to the percentage of votes they received. As a business owner, I could just have the bookkeeper send a check, or I could call the charities and say, "I'm doing this thing for you." But we want to operate out of humility in this area too. I thought it would be a good experience to have the members of my team who voted for each organization to contact them directly and let them know about the gift they're making.

Each group set up video calls with their organizations to tell them how much they were giving and the reason the team chose them. I wanted to step back and let my team have their own experience, so I sat in on one of these calls. This particular organization helps graduation rates in inner city schools, and they have been incredibly effective—graduation rates have improved from 60 to 95 percent. My team members explained why they had chosen to give money to an organization they had never come across until I gave them a description of what the group did and a link to their website. Their comments were so meaningful and expressive about what was tugging on their heart enough to say, "This is the one I want to give to."

For one of my team members, giving to this organization was deeply personal. He said, "I was raised by teenage parents. My dad was an alcoholic and left us when I was really young. My mom had a drug addiction during my childhood. I was a kid in the situation you're trying to help children out of. And so it was really important to me to see this money go to you." I didn't know about my team member's childhood. His transparency, honesty, openness, and willingness to share his experience with that organization had everyone on the video call moved to tears and motivated to do more. A few months later he became a dad … to twins! He will be a great father.

DON'T FORGET THE FINANCIALS

Although building a giving strategy is not going to be 100 percent about money, it will play a substantial role. The first thing to think about is how to create a budget. An organization like Generous Giving is a good resource to learn how to allocate funds in your annual budget. A financial planner can also be a resource to bring into your business and work with your finance team to set up a structure that creates a giving fund.

Look into the tax benefits of tithing. I find that many business leaders don't understand the strategy around taxes and tithes. There are some good tax strategies for giving that can help you build a scalable donation fund. Personally, I would rather take the cash and use that money to give than hand it over in taxes. Data shows that faith-based organizations are more effective at creating transformational change than government. When I develop a well-thought-out strategy, I know for a fact that the money is going to help heal our world. Working with a financial advisor gifted at developing these strategies will enable your business to set clear plans on how to get the most out of your giving. Ronald Blue Trust is one example, and they have great systems, leadership, and vision to guide your giving for optimal impact.

I also recommend planning your financials so that you can get your tithes made in a timely way, as close to the time you earned them as you can. I've seen good power in that. If you're not sure how you want to disperse the money you want to allocate, it's okay to put it into a donor-advised fund until a time when you are called to donate to somebody. It's like a checking account for your donations.

One of the things I've seen, though, is that people get too cautious about making sure they find the perfect organization or ministry to donate to. They want to do a ton of checking to determine the legitimacy and how the funds will be used. That is important research to do. But it's okay if you're called to be reckless with your giving as well. I think that gets blessed in an equal way. You want to make as many sound decisions as you can, but don't worry so much about being perfect. You'll end up paralyzing yourself and not get your tithing into the world to do what it's supposed to.

On the other side of that, don't hoard your charitable money and then windfall it onto one group. Try to disperse it to get as much impact as you can. I allocate my donations based on the type of impact it will have. I go with 50 percent local, 25 percent national, and 25 percent international. That's just where I'm at today. I'm not saying that this is the way you should do it. That's just one way of figuring out how much of your resources are distributed across those communities.

The last thing to remember about giving—and this is extremely important—is that you must release attachment to your gift. Assuming that you have made an informed decision and prayed for wisdom, make the decision to give, and then just let that money go. Expect nothing in return, such as recognition, a plaque, a parking spot, or a thank you. Just give. Holding any kind of attachment to that money will just bring pain and disappointment.

Choose How You Will Give

Monetary donations and gifts are always a good thing. But giving does not always have to involve cash. What you want to look at is time, talent, and treasure. Viewing giving through that lens, you have to consider things like service projects, board service, volunteering for nonprofits, and other donations of time and talent as sources of giving. A well-run board can get a lot out of a good businessperson who's giving. Board service is not only for the business owner but also for key leaders on a team who have a passion for different causes.

Someone with a good business mind can help a nonprofit board in many ways. They can bring their experience in how they run their business and advise the organization in some area of need, such as marketing, operations, finance, etc. All those things are sharable between a ministry and the businessperson. They can also open up their networks to a nonprofit and make connections between like-minded people who might be interested in being involved with what they're doing. They can invite people they know to events or share their experiences with a nonprofit or cause they work with. In doing this, the businessperson is helping the organization grow and is inviting others along on the journey.

Another way to consider time, talent, and treasure is to look at what your business does that can be donated to a cause. If you're in marketing, are there things you can do in social media that help a local women's shelter or humane society? If you're manufacturing shingles, is there a way that you can donate some product to Habitat for Humanity? Homes of Hope has benefited over the years from consulting work donated by Patrick Lencioni, who wrote *The Five Dysfunctions of a Team*. These are folks using the gift they bring to the world to help a ministry be able to move themselves forward.

Raise Money for Others

If you look at the world around us, the poor do not listen to the poor, and the rich do not listen to the poor. The poor and the rich listen to the rich. As you create more wealth, you carry more influence, and that influence is something you have stewardship over. You can give a lot of money to your cause. But you can also use your influence with other businesses, leaders, and colleagues to inspire them to give as well. Helping others raise money becomes important because you now have a relevant voice to influence others to open their hearts and wallets.

Defenders got involved with a program called School on Wheels. It's a program here in Indianapolis that brings resources like tutors and supplies to places where homeless kids are so that they can get help with their schoolwork. They also provide school uniforms and other supplies they might need. If you think about the life of a homeless child, you can imagine what kind of a gift it is just to have a place to study and a tutor to help with their homework. It's support they don't get outside of school, and the public school system can only provide so much for them during weekdays.

My son RJ participated in a service project we were doing with School on Wheels. He said to the whole group of us after we were back at the office, "I grew up in a rural environment, and we were never wealthy. There certainly were a lot of poor people in our county, but I never knew of anybody who was homeless. Then I get here, and I find out there's thirty-five hundred children homeless in Marion County every night. That was just overwhelming to me. It opened my eyes to how much need there is out there."

That single experience inspired him and other team members to tap their own networks and resources to raise over $35,000 so that School on Wheels could provide kids with free uniforms. The team and my son all have influence within their own circles of friends and contacts. When they tapped into those resources and used that influence, they were able to give a profoundly valuable gift to those children. Now imagine what you could do with all your vast resources.

Set Giving Goals

If you have a specific goal you're working toward, both as an individual and as a team, you have a mission that will keep you motivated to work toward until it's complete. I'll set a giving goal for myself personally before I'll set a goal for how much I want to make for a year. To put that first, you always want to have the goal be your top-of-mind thinking: this year, I'm going to give $200, $2,000, $20,000, $200,000, $2 million (whatever your goal might be). Break it down into monthly or quarterly goals. This helps to ensure that you will complete the mission.

Dave went on his first trip to build houses with Homes of Hope in Mexico just before Defenders' annual convention in 2008. We were backstage, and I was prepping him for delivering his speech to the whole company. He was distracted. I tried to keep his focus because we had only five minutes before showtime, and I needed him to know what to say and when. But he kept interrupting me. "Marcia, my life changed this week," he said. "I've been in Mexico on a mission trip, and my life is different today than it was before I left." Focused on the immediate issue, I said, "That's really nice and here is what's on the slides you're going to present." He didn't hear me. "No, listen," he said. "My wife and kids are never going to be the same again either. It was just an amazing experience! What would it be like if we sent every employee and their family on a mission trip to build a home for somebody in Mexico?"

I said to him (probably in a dismissive tone), "That's a beautiful idea. We don't have it in the financial plan today, so let's get through this convention, and on Monday we can start talking about how we can do that next year." He agreed that it wasn't a good idea to rush into it at this point. Then he went on stage to deliver his speech and announced to more than six hundred people that we're all going to Mexico to build houses. The crowd jumped to their feet in applause and cheers.

In that moment, he was a reckless giver. I was shaking my head backstage, wondering how in the heck we were going to do this. But I was given Dave's assignment to make this happen, ASAP. We developed a financial plan that would enable sixty-five managers and company leaders make the trip that fall. We built four homes in that program, and for many it was a life changing experience.

The second year, the plan was to build eight homes, and we budgeted for more folks to go on two missions. Homes of Hope had a lot of groups forgo their trips because the US was being hit hard with recession, swine flu, and travel bans. Mexico was also experiencing an increase in drug cartel violence. On our first trip that year, Dave pulled me over to speak with Sean Lambert, the founder of the program. Dave said, "This work they're doing is so important. With all these things in the economy, violence, and flu moving against them, they're really kind of in a tough spot. How many homes are we supposed to build this year?" I told him we were going to build eight homes according to the business plan and budget.

"Aren't revenues on track to hit above the sales plan we set for the year?" Dave asked me. I told him I expected that we would come in at double the goal. He said, "I think we can build more houses. How many do you think we can do?"

I thought that if we were going to double the business above the plan, it made sense to double the number of houses. "If we stretch, sixteen might be doable," I said.

"Sixteen is a good number," Dave replied. "Let's do thirty." Again, reckless giver.

That mission put us on a path that year to talk six hundred people—team members and their families—into going on these builds, in addition to doing our already hectic jobs and figuring out the financials to make these trips happen. It was a big ask, but it was a priority for Dave and the company. I hired another person to add to the leadership team who took much of the work for this project off my shoulders, Mike Lantz, our Chief Learning Officer, I put my voice and authority behind it, and we delivered the financials we needed to make everything work.

By the end of the year, we had built thirty-two homes. Now I'm not advocating that you take Dave's approach to goal setting. Putting more time and strategic thinking into setting your giving goals is much more practical. But this story is a good illustration of how when you have a specific mission—a calling—you can find a way to make it happen.

I hope you're still with me on this crazy journey of new ideas and perspectives toward marketing, leadership development, and growth. Because now I want something from you. I've openly shared with you my marketing model and the most valuable experiences I've had that have enabled me to find my own path to success. You're now in an excellent position to go into the world and create wealth. I want you to use that wealth to help other people transform, just like I have helped you. Make giving a big part of your business. Take my experiences and advice and run with them so that you can make this world a better place.

TOOLS FOR GROWTH

RESOURCES: THE JOY OF GIVING

Scan the QR code or visit mathbeforemarketing.com/stories

TOOLS FOR GROWTH

HARVESTING IDEAS

MY IDEAS FROM THIS CHAPTER

CONCLUSION

You will get all you want in life, if you help enough other people get what they want.

—ZIG ZIGLAR

A t age twenty-four, I read Zig Ziglar's book *See You at the Top*. On the first page, he wrote one thing in big bold print, shouting out a message to me that would change my life and thousands of others': "You will get all you want in life, if you help enough other people get what they want." I was immediately overwhelmed by all the memories of other people who had helped me in my life. The teachers, coaches, family members, 4-H leaders, church members, youth groups, choir … the list was long. God had put the right people in my path at just the right time to guide me. And I developed a deep desire in my heart to do the same for others.

> *Everything in my life, good or bad, has been an opportunity to learn, grow, serve others, create abundance, and thrive.*

Everything in my life, good or bad, has been an opportunity to learn, grow, serve others, create abundance, and thrive. There is one story to show the ripple effect that this journey creates. It brings together the incredible power to influence the world using the tools shared in this book.

In 2018, I invited my friends Sherry and Greg, along with their thirteen-year-old son, Alex, to join me on a Homes of Hope build. None of them had ever participated in anything like a Homes of Hope mission before. As expected, traveling out of the country to the most impoverished Mexican hillsides to build a home in two days will stretch most people's comfort zones. Alex had wanted to do a mission trip for years. He was a tall, quiet, introverted young man with a heart for the Lord and baseball. The only thing I knew Alex feared was public speaking.

On day one, the family arrived at the build site anxious to navigate the process of finishing a house for the Mexican family. As the team got started, Greg was happy to hammer away at the roof trusses and walls with Alex at his side. He had owned a successful construction company prior to his Parkinson's disease diagnosis, but his health had taken a physical toll on him. As the work began, his muscle memory took over, and he was once again joyfully sharing his gifts for building with his family and with the family for whom he was helping to build a house.

Sherry and I worked on the painting crew. She was so full of joy watching her family help another family. And while we were busy with the work, she kept an attentive eye on Alex, making sure that he was using sunscreen and staying hydrated—and reinforcing the ever-present reminder of hand sanitizer.

The night before the build, the missionaries had dropped off a portable toilet to the build site. These are also known as porta potties, outhouses, porta johns, port-a-lets, and my favorite, honey buckets. I hang out with a lot of missionaries, and I've always been curious about the one who answers God's call to serve the kingdom imagining teaching, translating, healing, and feeding people around the world and gets the job of dropping off and picking up the porta potties.

Late in the morning, nature called Alex and off he went to the toilet. A little while later, Alex came to his mom with his arm extended and holding his cell phone, both of which were dripping with blue gunk running down his arm all the way to the elbow.

"I dropped my cell phone in the porta potty," Alex said, not nearly as concerned as the rest of us about the gunk encasing his arm. Sherry and I looked at each other in wide-eyed panic. She ran for the water and disinfectant to wash all the blue stuff off Alex and the phone. Alex held fast to his belief that no one had yet used the porta potty from the build team. We knew that if you put a porta potty overnight in a village with no toilets or running water, people will use it. That gunk on Alex's arm and phone was most certainly not uncontaminated chemically treated water from public sanitation.

Needless to say, the phone wasn't working, and Alex became concerned about this aspect of the situation. Refusing to be shaken, Alex found a happy place in his theory about the cleanliness of the water and remained concerned only for the cell phone's return to life. He simply cleaned it and then set it in the sun to dry. After lunch, the phone started working again. Alex was so happy. He showed us all that it would still turn on, get signals, and receive messages. Our whole team laughed and joked with Alex all day about his own personal "rescue mission."

The next day, I delivered a teaching lesson for the builder groups and missionaries and, with Alex's permission, told everyone about his reckless cell phone rescue story. All two hundred of us were laughing together at this boy's audacity and innocence. With that reflection came a big question: Why did Alex plunge his arm, all the way up to the elbow, into a toilet bowl of chunky blue gunk to search for an easily replaceable phone? The answers were very simple: He wanted to send text messages. He didn't want to have to buy a new phone. He wanted to take pictures. He did not want to lose his saved pictures. He wanted to call his parents and friends. In short, Alex saw great value in that phone—so much so that he was willing to do something disgusting to see it restored for a purpose.

This story makes me think about God's love for me. My life has not been perfect. Whatever perceptions you may have of me before or after reading this book, the bottom line is that I make mistakes. Well, the truth is that I sin. At times, I have wandered far from God's design and desire for me to a place where my sins become greater, more frequent, more damaging. I have lied, gossiped, stolen, and hurt people. I've been greedy, proud, and arrogant. I've stepped out to the edge of totally losing any semblance of how I was created.

My sin is repugnant to God. He created me for something better. My neglect of his ways and forgetting who I am and how I've been created, separates me from God. To God, my sin is the same as the contents of a porta potty. And in my sin, I seem to sometimes be comfortable, staying in the crap like it's a Jacuzzi. Yet because God values me, he reaches into the blue gunk, through the crap, and lifts me out. He washes me whiter than snow and sets me in the Son. And when I've come out of my sinful state, he shouts throughout heaven, "She works! She can still receive messages! She can call me!"

The porta potty story made Alex a celebrity for the rest of the trip. You couldn't find a seat at his table for any meal. Everyone knew his name. Everyone wanted to talk to him about his experience. When we finished building the house, Alex was selected to give the Mexican family the keys to their new home. He delivered a profound message about God's love and generosity that moved us all to tears.

That evening, Alex picked up a microphone and spoke to the group about what he was learning about God, Mexico, his family, and himself. This boy who came to Mexico fearing public speaking did not bat an eye standing in front of hundreds of people and teaching them something about his experience. When he returned home, Alex had grown in faith, compassion, courage, and leadership. He shared his story about the cell phone, the porta potty, and God's love for us with his baseball team, schoolmates, family, and friends.

Two years later, the cell phone did get replaced, and Greg built a frame for it. The phone hangs in their home as a cherished memory and great conversation starter. I imagine someday that Greg and Sherry will hold grandchildren on their laps while Alex says, "Let me tell you about God's love for us …"

This book is a map to experiencing your own Alex stories. Not just one but as many as you can. I'm excited to be on this journey with you and look forward to hearing what is being created in and through your application of these tools I've shared.

Here we grow!

PICTURED: GREG, SHERRY, AND ALEX

ADDITIONAL RESOURCES

TOOLS FOR GROWTH

FREE: MARKETING ASSESSMENT
Scan the QR code or visit mathbeforemarketing.com/free

TOOLS FOR GROWTH

10X CALCULATOR
Scan the QR code or visit mathbeforemarketing.com/tenx

TOOLS FOR GROWTH

MARCIA'S LIST: GROWTH PARTNERS
Scan the QR code or visit mathbeforemarketing.com/partners

CPSIA information can be obtained
at www.ICGtesting.com
Printed in the USA
JSHW011546030723
44165JS00006B/119